SEARCH, PONDER, and PLAY with

SUPER
SCRIPTURE ACTIVITIES

| Jesus Is My Friend |

Fun-to-Make Visuals ○ SEARCH and PONDER Cards
Show-and-Tell Presentations ○ Games and Activities
Primary Songs ○ Favors and Prizes ○ Thought Treats
Scripture Activity Invitations ○ Bonus Motivators

JESUS IS MY FRIEND

ACTIVITY THEMES:

THE BLESSED BEATITUDES:
Jesus Gave the Sermon on the Mount

SERVICE WITH A SMILE:
Jesus Performed Miracles

CAPTAIN OF OUR SHIP:
Jesus Is Our Life Savior

Copyright © 1995 by Mary H. Ross and Jennette Guymon
All Rights Reserved

Covenant Communications, Inc.
American Fork, Utah

Printed in the United States of America
First Printing: August 1995

95 96 97 98 99 00 01   10 9 8 7 6 5 4 3 2 1

Super Scripture Activities: Jesus Is My Friend

ISBN 1-55503-861-1

INTRODUCTION

Jesus Is My Friend

Too often in today's world, videos and television replace scripture reading programs, and children grow up not knowing the real stories from the scriptures. But now there's a great way to beat the competition!

In this useful and entertaining volume, you'll find New Testament activities to make learning fun.

Use Activities For:
- ♥ Family Home Evening
- ♥ Primary Sharing Time
- ♥ Classroom Presentations
- ♥ 2 1/2 Minute Talks
- ♥ Daily Devotionals
- ♥ Achievement Days
- ♥ Young Women
- ♥ and more

At home or in the classroom, any day can be a scripture-reading fun day with these theme-coordinated activities. Everything is planned for you, with patterns ready to copy and enjoy. Just choose the activities that suit your individual needs, or combine activities to enjoy a SUPER SCRIPTURE ACTIVITY.

This volume offers a variety of exciting New Testament themes for your study and enjoyment. Each fun, information-filled section stimulates an interest in the scriptures, and includes activities to entertain and delight. It is designed to help children gain a testimony of Jesus Christ and learn to live as he did.

Using the materials presented here, you'll be able to choose from many activities to enhance your New Testament course of study. SEARCH and PONDER the scriptures, and then PLAY: Have fun with activities that reinforce scripture learning. Each activity helps you better understand the scriptures and make them part of your life.

SUPPLIES ARE SIMPLE: Pattern copies, scissors, crayons or markers, tape, glue, string, simple craft supplies, and Thought Treats

CHOOSE FROM THE FOLLOWING ACTIVITIES AS YOU
SEARCH, PONDER, AND PLAY:

SEARCH and PONDER

- ☐ SEARCH & PONDER cards help you SEARCH the scriptures to find missing words, and PONDER scripture questions.
- ☐ SCRIPTURE SHOW-AND-TELL with pictures to color and present with cue cards.

PLAY: SUPER SCRIPTURE ACTIVITY Choices

- ☐ SCRIPTURE SHOW-AND-TELL presentations.
- ☐ GAMES or ACTIVITIES to make learning fun.
- ☐ SONGS from the Children's Songbook* are suggested.
- ☐ FAVOR and PRIZE patterns are ready to copy, cut and paste.
- ☐ THOUGHT TREATS to sweeten the appetite for more scripture reading.
- ☐ INVITATIONS to invite guests to a SUPER SCRIPTURE ACTIVITY featuring choices above.
- ☐ BONUS MOTIVATORS to reward guests for completing the Search and Ponder cards.

*Children's Songbook, CD, and cassette tapes are published by The Church of Jesus Christ of Latter-day Saints, Salt Lake City, Utah.

Jesus Is My Friend

TABLE OF CONTENTS

> Super Scripture Activity Theme #1
>
> **THE BLESSED BEATITUDES: Sermon on the Mount**

Scripture Activity Checklist 1

Invitation
Buzz on Over for a Blessed Bee-atitude Scripture Activity!
  (bee bag to collect honey taffy and Bee-atitude puzzle) 2

SEARCH and PONDER

Search and Ponder cards 3-4
SERMON ON THE MOUNT BEATITUDES:
- Poor in Spirit   ○ They That Mourn   ○ Meek Inherit Earth
- Hunger After Righteousness   ○ Pure in Heart   ○ Peacemakers
- Persecuted for Right

PLAY

Scripture Show-and-Tell presentations
Blessed Beatitudes: Jesus Gave Sermon on the Mount bee poster
  (with matching pictures and cue cards) 5-8, 12-19

Game
Bee-atitude Blockbuster quiz game
  (two blocks with beatitudes to fill in missing words) 9, 20-21

Favors and Prizes
Bee-atitude dot match puzzle 10, 22
Honey Buzz Taffy* 10

Thought Treats
*Honey Buzz Taffy (Bee-atitude Blockbuster game prize) 10
Bee-atitude Bagels (with bee sign and cream cheese spread) 11

Bonus Motivators (reward for completing Search and Ponder cards)
Bee-atitude one-a-day goal cards to tape on mirror 23-24

> Super Scripture Activity Theme #2
>
> # SERVICE WITH A SMILE: Jesus Performed Miracles

Scripture Activity Checklist 25

Invitation
You're Invited to a Service with a Smile Activity 26

SEARCH and PONDER

Search and Ponder cards 27-28
Jesus Healed a Man Who Could Not Walk
Jesus Commanded the Wind and the Waves
Jesus Fed 5,000 People
Jesus Walked on Water
Jesus Raised Lazarus to Life
Jesus Healed Ten Lepers

PLAY

Scripture Show-and-Tell presentations
Service with a Smile: Jesus Performed Miracles poster
 (with matching pictures and cue cards) 29-32, 36-44

Game
Go the Extra Mile: Show Service with a Smile match game 33, 45-48

Favors and Prizes
Service with a Smile visor 34, 49
Go the Extra Mile: Show Service with a Smile medallion 34, 50
Service with a Smile coupon book 34, 51-52

Thought Treats
Service Snacks (chips and olives) 35, 53
Super Smile Cookies 35

Bonus Motivators (rewards for completing service and Search and Ponder cards)
Service with a Smile certificate and glue-on stickers 54

Super Scripture Activity Theme #3

CAPTAIN OF OUR SHIP: Jesus Is Our Life Savior

Scripture Activity Checklist 55

Invitation
Ahoy! Sail on Over for a SCRIPTURE ACTIVITY! 56

SEARCH and PONDER

Search and Ponder cards 57-58
Jesus Enters Jerusalem: The Pharisees Plot to Kill Him
Jesus and the Apostles: Sacrament and the Last Supper
Jesus Suffers for Our Sins in the Garden of Gethsemane
Jesus Is Crucified and Forgives His Enemies
Jesus Is Resurrected: He Is Our Life Savior
Jesus Says Farewell and Sends the Holy Ghost: He Will Return

PLAY

Scripture Show-and-Tell presentations
Captain of Our Ship: Jesus Is Our Life Savior ship scene
   (with matching pictures and cue cards) 59-62, 66-74

Game
S.O.S. Save Our Ship: Jesus Is Our Life Savior match game 63, 75-80

Favors and Prizes
I Can Sail Through the Storms of Life sailor hat 64, 81
My Life Can Be Ship-Shape bookmark 64, 82

Thought Treats
Save Our Ship Submarine Sandwich
   (with ship toothpick sign) 65, 83
Jesus Is Our Life Savior doughnut
   (with tag tied to doughnut with strawberry candy rope) 65, 84

Bonus Motivators (rewards for completing Search and Ponder cards)
Good Show Sailor! medal of honor 85

PLACE ACTIVITIES IN FILE FOLDER: Cut out and mount label and checklist on folder. →↓

New Testament
Blessed Beatitudes:
Jesus Gave the Sermon on the Mount

SCRIPTURE ACTIVITY CHECKLIST
Blessed Beatitudes: Jesus Gave the Sermon on the Mount

PAGES:

Let's get an attitude towards the beatitudes, that Jesus gave during his Sermon on the Mount. The beatitudes are things we can do to get to heaven, things that will make us happy, like *"Blessed are the pure in heart: for they shall see God."* (Matthew 5:8)

Jesus gave nine blessings in Matthew 5:3-12. They all start with a good attitude. Think as Jesus thought. Think of the happiness that can come from living his teachings.

Remember: You can't <u>beat</u> a good <u>attitude</u>, so BE A BEE-ATITUDE BELIEVER.

DO AHEAD:
- ☐ Copy patterns ... 11-24
- ☐ Create Invitation or Favor: Bee-atitude beehive with honey taffy and puzzle prizes 2, 10
- ☐ Gather supplies*

PAGES:

SEARCH and PONDER:

- ☐ SEARCH & PONDER cards 3-4
- ☐ SCRIPTURE SHOW-AND-TELL: Rehearse cue cards for presentation: Buzz on Over to Heaven's Beehive poster 5-8

PLAY: SUPER SCRIPTURE ACTIVITY Choices

- ☐ SCRIPTURE SHOW-AND-TELL presentation
- ☐ GAME: Bee-atitude Blockbuster quiz game 9
- ☐ ACTIVITY: Bee-atitude dot match puzzle (prize for game) 10
- ☐ SONGS:
  - ○ "Tell Me the Stories of Jesus," page 57**
  - ○ "Choose the Right Way," page 160**
  - ○ "I Will Follow God's Plan," page 164**
  - ○ "Teach Me to Walk in the Light," page 177**

*SUPPLIES: Pattern copies, scissors, crayons or markers, zip-close plastic sandwich bag, double-stick tape, and Thought Treats

- ☐ FAVORS and PRIZES: 10
  - ○ Bee-atitude dot match puzzle (activity)
  - ○ Honey Buzz Taffy
- ☐ THOUGHT TREATS: 10-11
  - ○ Bee-atitude Bagels with bee sign
  - ○ Honey Bee Cream Cheese Spread
- ☐ BONUS MOTIVATORS: 23-24

SUPPLEMENTAL READING--New Testament Stories**: The Sermon on the Mount

**Children's Songbook and New Testament Stories are published by The Church of Jesus Christ of Latter-day Saints, Salt Lake City, Utah.

Blessed Beatitudes: Jesus Gave Sermon on the Mount

PATTERN: "Buzz on over" invitation to enclose in a zip-close plastic sandwich bag.

TO MAKE:
1. Copy invitation below for each guest on yellow or gold cardstock paper.
2. Color and cut out invitation.
3. Fill in invitation details.
4. Slip invitation inside a zip-close bag. Guests are instructed to bring the bag to the activity to collect something sweet. We suggest the following:

♥ **THOUGHT TREAT:** Honey Buzz Taffy (see page 10)

♥ **FAVOR OR PRIZE:** Bee-atitude dot match puzzle (see page 10)

Scripture SEARCH and PONDER:

♥ Copy two sets of SEARCH and PONDER cards below on colored cardstock paper. ♥ Cut out cards.
- Use Set #1 for Daily Devotionals.
- OPTION: Make a second set of cards to play The New Testament Game--Spotlighting the Life of Jesus. (This game is found on pages 59-60 of SUPER SCRIPTURE ACTIVITIES--NEW TESTAMENT, by Mary H. Ross and Jennette Guymon. Copy each set of cards a different color to identify quickly, i.e. copy this set bright gold.)

SEARCH #1
Blessed Beatitudes

Sermon on the Mount
Beatitude: Poor in Spirit

"And seeing the multitudes, he went up into a mountain: and when he was set, his disciples came unto him: And he opened his mouth, and taught them, saying, Blessed are the poor in spirit (who come unto me*): for theirs is the kingdom of

_ _ _ _ _ _ _."
(Matthew 5:1-3)
(*3 Nephi 12:3)

SEARCH #2
Blessed Beatitudes

Sermon on the Mount
Beatitude: They That Mourn
Beatitude: Meek Inherit Earth

"Blessed are they that mourn: for they shall be
_ _ _ _ _ _ _ _ _."
(Matthew 5:4)
....

"Blessed are the meek: for they shall _ _ _ _ _ _ _ the earth."
(Matthew 5:5)

SEARCH #3
Blessed Beatitudes

Sermon on the Mount
Beatitude: Hunger After Right
Beatitude: Merciful

"Blessed are they which do hunger and thirst after righteousness; for they shall be
_ _ _ _ _ _ (with the Holy Ghost*)."
(Matthew 5:6) (*3 Nephi 12:6)
....

"Blessed are the merciful: for they shall obtain
_ _ _ _ _."
(Matthew 5:7)

SEARCH #4
Blessed Beatitudes

Sermon on the Mount
Beatitude: Pure in Heart
Beatitude: Peacemakers

"Blessed are the pure in heart: for they shall see _ _ _."
(Matthew 5:8)
....

"Blessed are the peacemakers: for they shall be called the
_ _ _ _ _ _ _ _ of God." (Matthew 5:9)

SEARCH #5
Blessed Beatitudes

Sermon on the Mount
Beatitude: Persecuted for Right

"Blessed are they which are persecuted for righteousness' (for my name*) _ _ _ _: for theirs is the kingdom of heaven." (Matthew 5:10)
(*3 Nephi 12:10)

SEARCH #6
Blessed Beatitudes

Sermon on the Mount
Beatitude: Persecuted for Right

"Blessed are ye, when men shall revile you, and persecute you, and shall say all manner of

_ _ _ _ _ against you falsely, for my sake.

Rejoice, and be exceedingly glad: for great is your
_ _ _ _ _ _ _ in heaven: for so persecuted they the prophets which were before you." (Matthew 5:11-12)

Blessed Beatitudes: Jesus Gave the Sermon on the Mount

PATTERNS: PONDER Cards #1-6

PONDER #1
Blessed Beatitudes

Sermon on the Mount
Beatitude: Poor in Spirit

What do you have to do if you are poor in spirit and you want to live in the kingdom of heaven?
(Matthew 5:1-3)

Come _ _ _ me [Jesus].
(see 3 Nephi 12:3)

This means repent and choose the right.

PONDER #2
Blessed Beatitudes

Sermon on the Mount
Beatitude: They That Mourn
Beatitude: Meek Inherit Earth

What happens to those who mourn, who are sad for those they have lost? (Matthew 5:4) They shall be (at peace)
_ _ _ _ _ _ _ _ _ _.

If you don't think you are better than other people, what are you? (Matthew 5:5)
_ _ _ _ (It means to be humble, patient, long-suffering.)

PONDER #3
Blessed Beatitudes

Sermon on the Mount
Beatitude: Hunger After Right
Beatitude: Merciful

How can we hunger and thirst after righteousness? State your opinion.
_____
_____

If we forgive others, will Heavenly Father forgive us?
(Matthew 5:7)

Yes ___ No ___

PONDER #4
Blessed Beatitudes

Sermon on the Mount
Beatitude: Pure in Heart
Beatitude: Peacemakers

What does it mean to be pure in heart? State your opinion.
(Matthew 5:8)
_____
_____

How should we love other people, and help them love each other? State your opinion.
(Matthew 5:9)
_____
_____

PONDER #5
Blessed Beatitudes

Sermon on the Mount
Beatitude: Persecuted for Right

Why is the kingdom of heaven promised to those who are persecuted for doing right? State your opinion.
(Matthew 5:10)
_____
_____

PONDER #6
Blessed Beatitudes

Sermon on the Mount
Beatitude: Persecuted for Right

If you are persecuted, how are you like the prophets which were before you?
(Matthew 5:11-12)

They were also
_ _ _ _ _ _ _ _ _ _.

Blessed Beatitudes: Jesus Gave the Sermon on the Mount

Scripture Show-and-Tell

Blessed Beatitudes: Jesus Gave Sermon on the Mount poster
- ♥ Copy and cut out cue cards that follow.
- ♥ Copy and cut out beehive and bees #1-11 (patterns on pages 12-19).

All patterns can be posted on a board or poster paper (see layout below).

SEARCH, PONDER, and PLAY

PRESENTATION PLAN:
Cards #1-6

SHOW: beehive and bees   TELL: Cue Cards #1-6

Scripture Show-and-Tell
Blessed Beatitudes

GIANT Beehive
Bee #1 Poor in Spirit Bee .... Card #1

Bee #2 Mourning Bee
Bee #3 Meek Bee .... Card #2

Bee #4 Righteous Bee
Bee #5 Merciful Bee .... Card #3

Bee #6 Pure in Heart Bee
Bee #7 Peacemaker Bee .... Card #4

Bee #8 Persecuted for Right Bee
Bee #9 Light Bee .... Card #5

Bee #10 Teacher Bee
Bee #11 Love Bee .... Card #6

♥ CUT outside line of both cards--DON'T cut center lines. ♥ Fold between center line to CREATE A FOLDER to store cards #1-6.

Blessed Beatitudes: Jesus Gave the Sermon on the Mount

CUT OUT cards #1-6 to rehearse Show-and-Tell presentation.

SEARCH, PONDER, and PLAY
Bee a Beatitude Believer - Bee #1 Poor in Spirit

Place giant beehive on board and say:

Scripture Show-and-Tell
Cue Card #1
Blessed Beatitudes

One day, Jesus taught thousands of people at one time. This was called the Sermon on the Mount. He told the people how they could get to heaven, by giving them the beatitudes and other words of wisdom. The beatitudes tell us how to be perfect. Each has a blessing that comes from obedience.

Jesus said, "*Be ye therefore perfect, even as your Father which is in Heaven is perfect.*" (Matthew 5:48) Jesus taught us to BEE PERFECT, so let's build a beehive and learn to bee-have, so we can buzz to heaven's beehive. Let these bees tell you how being a Beatitude Believer can buzz you closer to heaven.

Place Bee #1 (Poor in Spirit) on board and say:

I am Poor in Spirit Bee. I am looking for the kingdom of heaven. Jesus told me: "*Blessed are the poor in spirit, (who come unto me*) for theirs is the kingdom of heaven.*" (Matthew 5:3) (*3 Nephi 12:3) Jesus said that if I am poor in spirit, and I come unto him, then I will be a part of his kingdom.

I WILL LISTEN AND "BEE" AS JESUS WOULD HAVE ME "BEE".

SEARCH, PONDER, and PLAY
Bee #2 (Mourning) and Bee #3 (Meek)

Place Bee #2 (Mourn) on board and say:

Scripture Show-and-Tell
Cue Card #2
Blessed Beatitudes

I am called Mourning Bee. Mourn means to be sad. I am sad, and I am looking for comfort.

Jesus told me: "*Blessed are they that mourn: for they shall be comforted.*" Ahh, it feels so nice to know that I have a loving Father in Heaven who wishes to care for me.

I BUZZ LOVE AND COMFORT TO OTHERS, AS HEAVENLY FATHER COMFORTS ME.

Place Bee #3 (Meek) on board and say:

I am known as Meek Bee. I try to be gentle with others. I am long-suffering, patient, and tolerant.

Jesus promised me, saying: "*Blessed are the meek: for they shall inherit the earth.*" This means that I will have many blessings while I am on this earth. This is true, as I have many blessings.

I WILL "BEE" LONG-SUFFERING, BUZZ KIND WORDS, "BEE" PATIENT AND UNDERSTAND.

Scripture Show-and-Tell
Cue Card #3
Blessed Beatitudes

SEARCH, PONDER, and PLAY

Bee #4 (Righteous) and Bee #5 (Merciful)

Place Bee #4 (Righteous) on board and say:

I am Righteous Bee. I try to choose the right each day. I help my neighbor and I pray.

Jesus said: "Blessed are they which do hunger and thirst after righteousness: for they shall be filled [with the Holy Ghost*]" (Matthew 5:6) (*3 Nephi 12:6) I have a strong desire to read the scriptures each day, so I can learn the righteous way.

I WILL "BEE" GOOD.

Place Bee #5 (Merciful) on board and say:

I am Merciful Bee. I am thoughtful of others. If someone is hurt, I try to help them. I have what you call compassion. I feel sorry for those who are in need, and help where I can.

Jesus promised me, saying: "Blessed are the merciful: for they shall obtain mercy." (Matthew 5:7) This means that if I show kindness to others, someone will be kind to me when I am in need.

I WILL BUZZ OVER TO HELP SOMEONE.

Scripture Show-and-Tell
Cue Card #4
Blessed Beatitudes

SEARCH, PONDER, and PLAY

Bee #5 (Pure in Heart) and Bee #6 (Peacemaker)

Place Bee #5 (Pure in Heart) on board and say:

I am Pure in Heart bee. My friends call me the straight arrow, because I like to do precisely the right thing. My thoughts are honest, and my actions are straightforward. You know what I am thinking and doing.

Jesus said: *"Blessed are the pure in heart: for they shall see God."* (Matthew 5:8) I'm trying to be like Jesus.

LET'S BUZZ THE STRAIGHT AND NARROW PATH.

Place Bee #6 (Peacemaker) on board and say:

I am Peacemaker Bee. Whenever there is fighting, or someone hurts someone else, I am there to help them feel calm. I try to find out what the problem is, and get help.

Jesus promised me, saying: *"Blessed are the peacemakers: for they shall be called the children of God."* (Matthew 5:9)   **I WILL "BEE" PEACEFUL WITH MY FAMILY AND FRIENDS, AND "BEE" A GOOD NEIGHBOR.**

SEARCH, PONDER, and PLAY
Bee #7 (Persecuted For Right) and Bee #8 (Light)

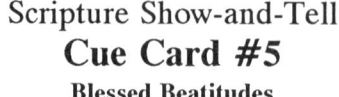

Scripture Show-and-Tell
Cue Card #5
Blessed Beatitudes

Place Bee #8 (Persecuted for Right) on board and say:

I am Persecuted for Right Bee. I try to do what is right, and make right choices. Sometimes others are mean to me and treat me bad. They say I should be doing the things they are doing. But those things are not right.

Jesus said: *"Blessed are they which are persecuted for righteousness' sake: for theirs is the kingdom of heaven."* (Matthew 5:10) I know that my reward will be in heaven, and not always on this earth.

I WILL BUZZ "NO" TO WRONG CHOICES.

Place Bee #9 (Light) on board and say:

I am called Light Bee. I try to shine brightly. I do not hide my light. I let it shine, so others can see that I am a good worker bee. When they see good works, they can feel closer to heaven's beehive.

Jesus said: *"Ye are the light of the world ... light a candle ... on a candlestick ... let your light so shine ..."* (Matthew 5:14-16)

I WILL BUZZ BRIGHT TOWARD HEAVEN'S LIGHT.

SEARCH, PONDER, and PLAY
Bee #9 (teacher) and Bee #10 (love)

Scripture Show-and-Tell
Cue Card #6
Blessed Beatitudes

Place Bee #10 (Teacher) on board and say:

I am called Teacher Bee. I teach others to do what is right. Jesus said that we should <u>not</u> teach others to break these commandments. He said: *"Whosoever ... shall break one of these ... commandments, and shall teach men so, he shall be called the least in the kingdom of heaven: but whosoever shall do and TEACH them, the same shall be called GREAT in the kingdom of heaven."* (Matthew 5:19) This means if I encourage my friends to do wrong, then I am teaching them wrong, and I will not have a high place in the beehive on high. I must teach them to do right. **I WILL BUZZ A MESSAGE TO OTHERS TO CHOOSE THE RIGHT.**

Place Bee #11 (love) on board and say:

I am Love Bee. I love everyone, even my enemies. Jesus said: *"Love your enemies, bless them that curse you, do good to them that hate you, and pray for them which despitefully use you, and persecute you; that ye may be the children of your Father which is in heaven."* (Matthew 5:44-45) **I WILL LOVE OTHERS AS JESUS DID, AND BUZZ TO MY HEAVENLY HIVE.**

SEARCH, PONDER, and PLAY

Bee-atitude Blockbuster quiz game

GAME
Blessed Beatitudes

OBJECTIVE:
Learn the beatitudes by guessing the missing words written on beatitude blocks.

YOU'LL NEED:
Copies of patterns on pages 20-21 on colored cardstock paper, scissors, crayons or markers, glue, and tape (one set of blocks per five guests).

HOW TO MAKE Bee-atitude Blocks:
1. Color the bees on each block.
2. Cut out blocks.
3. Fold and glue edges, and tape down lid.

HOW TO PLAY GAME:
Play with teams or with 2-5 players.
1. Take turns rolling one block at a time, alternating blocks.
2. Play for Points: The first player who earns

100 POINTS TO WIN!

◘ **10 POINTS:** Land on Bee-atitude Blessing and find the missing word in scriptures.
◘ **20 POINTS:** Guess the missing word.
◘ **20 POINTS:** Land on Bee-atitude Blockbuster.
◘ **20 POINTS:** Land on Buzz Your Way to Heaven.

Favors or Prizes:
#1 Honey Buzz Taffy (see recipe on page 10)
#2 Bee-atitude dot match puzzle (see page 2)

SEARCH, PONDER, and PLAY

BEE-ATITUDE dot match puzzle

ACTIVITY and Favor or PRIZE
Blessed Beatitudes

OBJECTIVE: Review the beatitudes Jesus taught in the Sermon on the Mount. Each bee-atitude is in a honeycomb shape.

STORAGE BAG FOR PUZZLE: Enclose this Bee-atitude dot match puzzle in a plastic bag* given to guests if they were invited to the SUPER SCRIPTURE ACTIVITY (invitation insert was placed in bag, detailed on page 2). Guests were instructed to bring bag to activity to collect honey treats (also enclose Honey Buzz Taffy detailed below).

YOU'LL NEED: Copy of bee-atitude dot match puzzle on page 22, scissors and crayons
(*Supply zip-close plastic bag for puzzle pieces if invitations were not sent.)

HOW TO MAKE & PUT TOGETHER PUZZLE:
Color and cut out puzzle pieces. Match up circles, dots and hearts on all sides.

SEARCH, PONDER, and PLAY

HONEY BUZZ TAFFY:
(Bee-atitude Blockbuster game prize)

PRIZES and TREATS
Blessed Beatitudes
Matthew 5:1-12

OBJECTIVE: Honey reminds us that heaven is sweet. Jesus gave us the bee-atitudes to show us the sweetest way to heaven.

YOU'LL NEED: One cup honey, and waxed paper (makes 35 pieces).

HOW TO MAKE TAFFY: ♥ Cook honey to boil stage and cook on medium heat 7-10 minutes, stirring often.
♥ Test for crackle stage. Drop 1/2 teaspoon of boiling honey into 1/2 cup of cold water. If medium ball forms, it's done. ♥ Butter a surface and pour honey onto surface to cool 3 minutes. ♥ Pull taffy with buttered fingers until light and porous. ♥ Cut into pieces and wrap with waxed paper.

SEARCH, PONDER, and PLAY

BEE-ATITUDE BAGLES
(with bee sign and cream cheese spread)

THOUGHT TREAT
Blessed Beatitudes
Matthew 5:1-12

YOU'LL NEED: Copy of "'Bee' a Buzzy Bee-atitude Believer" sign below on cardstock paper, toothpicks, bagels, cream cheese spread for each bagel. **RECIPE:** Mix 1/2 part cream cheese with 1/2 part honey.
HOW TO MAKE BEE-ATITUDE BAGLES: Cut bagel in half, spread cream cheese over each half (to make two servings). Insert sign with toothpick.
ACTIVITY: Read a beatitude from Matthew 5:1-12 and say: "Bee a buzzy bee-atitude believer."

Blessed Beatitudes: Jesus Gave the Sermon on the Mount

Blessed Beatitudes: Jesus Gave the Sermon on the Mount

Blessed Beatitudes: Jesus Gave the Sermon on the Mount

Blessed Beatitudes: Jesus Gave the Sermon on the Mount

Blessed Beatitudes: Jesus Gave the Sermon on the Mount

Blessed Beatitudes: Jesus Gave the Sermon on the Mount

17

Blessed Beatitudes: Jesus Gave the Sermon on the Mount

Blessed Beatitudes: Jesus Gave the Sermon on the Mount

Blessed Beatitudes: Jesus Gave the Sermon on the Mount

PATTERN: Bee-atitude Blockbuster block #1 for game ♥ Copy on cardstock paper.

Blessed Beatitudes: Jesus Gave the Sermon on the Mount

PATTERN: Bee-atitude Blockbuster block #2 for game ♥ Copy on cardstock paper.

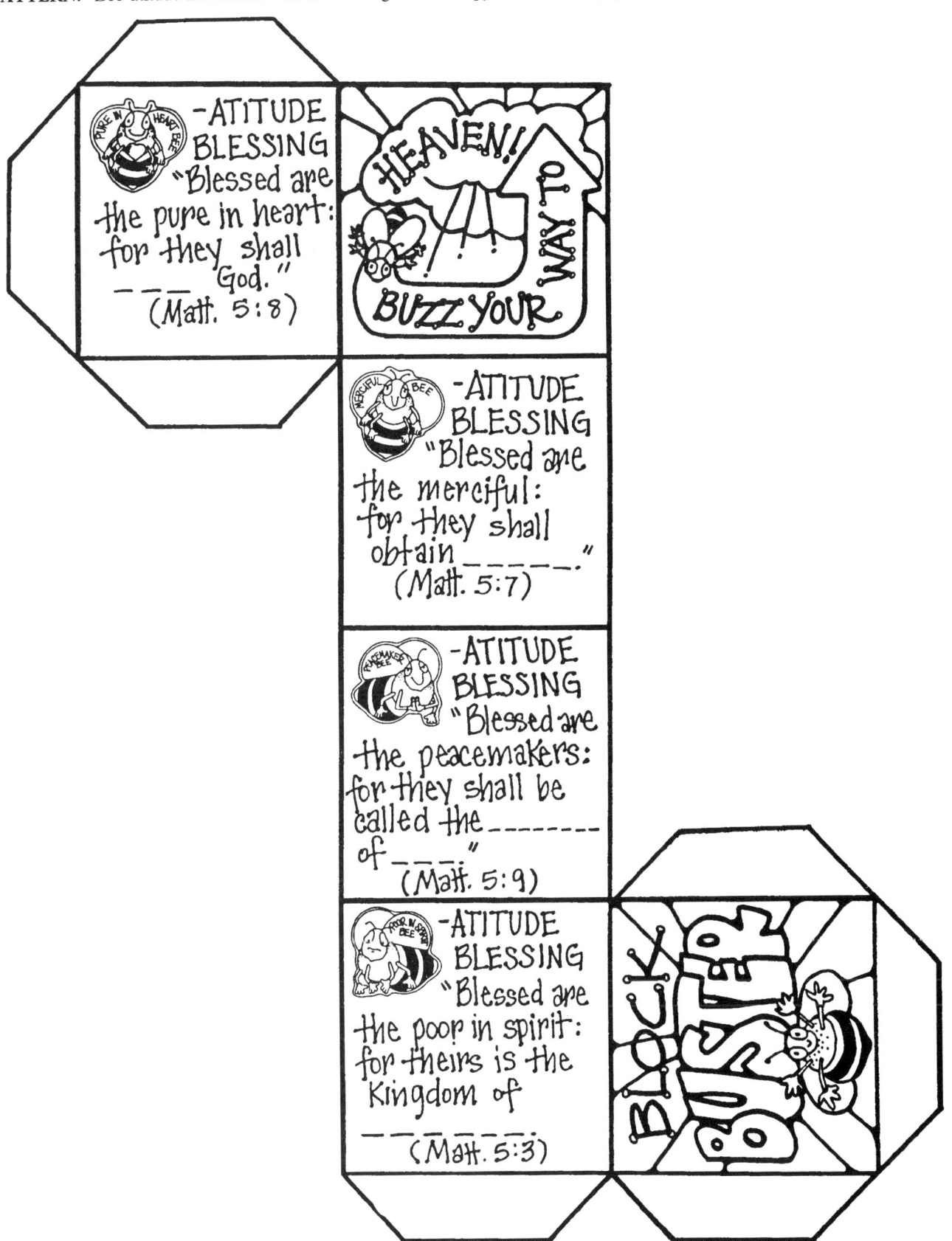

21

Blessed Beatitudes: Jesus Gave the Sermon on the Mount

Blessed Beatitudes: Jesus Gave the Sermon on the Mount

PATTERN: Bee-atitude one-a-day goal cards to tape on mirror (BONUS MOTIVATORS for completing the "Blessed Beatitudes" Search and Ponder cards) ♥ Copy on yellow or gold cardstock paper for each guest.

I am Meek Bee

I will "bee" long-suffering, buzz kind words, "bee" patient, and "bee" understanding to others.
Matthew 5:5

I am Righteous Bee

I will "bee" good.
Matthew 5:6 and 3 Nephi 12:6

I am Merciful Bee

I will buzz over to help someone.
Matthew 5:7

I am Pure in Heart Bee

I will buzz the straight and narrow path to heaven.
Matthew 5:8

Blessed Beatitudes: Jesus Gave the Sermon on the Mount

PATTERN: Bee-atitude one-a-day goal cards to tape on mirror (BONUS MOTIVATORS for completing the "Blessed Beatitudes" Search and Ponder cards) ♥ Copy on yellow or gold cardstock paper for each guest.

I am Peacemaker Bee

I will "bee" peaceful with my family and friends, and "bee" a good neighbor.
Matthew 5:9

I am Light Bee

I will buzz bright toward heaven's light.
Matthew 5:14-16

I am Teacher Bee

I will buzz a message to others to choose the right.
Matthew 5:19

I am Love Bee

I will love others as Jesus did, and buzz to my heavenly hive.
Matthew 5:44-45

PLACE ACTIVITIES IN FILE FOLDER: Cut out and mount label and checklist on folder.

New Testament
Service with a Smile:
Jesus Performed Miracles

SCRIPTURE ACTIVITY CHECKLIST
Service with a Smile: Jesus Performed Miracles

PAGES:

Let's follow Jesus and learn how to show SERVICE WITH A SMILE.

Jesus came to earth to show us how to help others. He healed the sick, calmed the seas, walked on water, and cured lepers of disease.

Let's follow the path that Jesus walked; let's not just sit and talk. He led the way, he walked that mile; he showed us SERVICE WITH A SMILE.

DO AHEAD:
- ☐ Copy patterns 36-54
- ☐ Create Invitation or Favor: Service With a Smile ... 26
- ☐ Gather supplies*

PAGES:

SEARCH and PONDER:

- ☐ SEARCH & PONDER cards 27-28
- ☐ SCRIPTURE SHOW-AND-TELL: Rehearse cue cards for presentation: Service With a Smile: Jesus Performed Miracles 29-32

PLAY: SUPER SCRIPTURE ACTIVITY Choices

- ☐ SCRIPTURE SHOW-AND-TELL presentation
- ☐ GAME: Go the Extra Mile: Show Service With a Smile match game 33
- ☐ SONGS:
  - ○ "I Am a Child of God," page 2**
  - ○ "Kindness Begins With Me," page 145**
  - ○ "When We're Helping," page 198**
  - ○ "I Feel My Savior's Love," page 74**
  - ○ "Go the Second Mile," page 167**
- ☐ FAVORS and PRIZES: 34
  - ○ SERVICE WITH A SMILE visor, medallion, and coupon book
- ☐ THOUGHT TREATS: 35
  - ○ Service Snacks: chips and olives
  - ○ Super Smile Cookies
- ☐ BONUS MOTIVATORS 54

*SUPPLIES: Pattern copies, scissors, crayons or markers, stapler, paper punch, string or ribbon, and Thought Treats

SUPPLEMENTAL READING--New Testament Stories**: The Man Who Could Not Walk, JESUS: Commands the Wind and the Waves, Feeds 5,000 People, Walks on the Water, Heals a Deaf Man and a Blind Man, Brings Lazarus Back to Life, and The Ten Lepers

**Children's Songbook and New Testament Stories are published by The Church of Jesus Christ of Latter-day Saints, Salt Lake City, Utah.

Service with a Smile: Jesus Performed Miracles

PATTERN: Service with a Smile invitation
♥ Copy on colored cardstock paper. Fold before cutting out invitation.
Cut on side (rounded) tabs. Fill in invitation details. Fold up so smile meets and hook bottom fold under tabs.

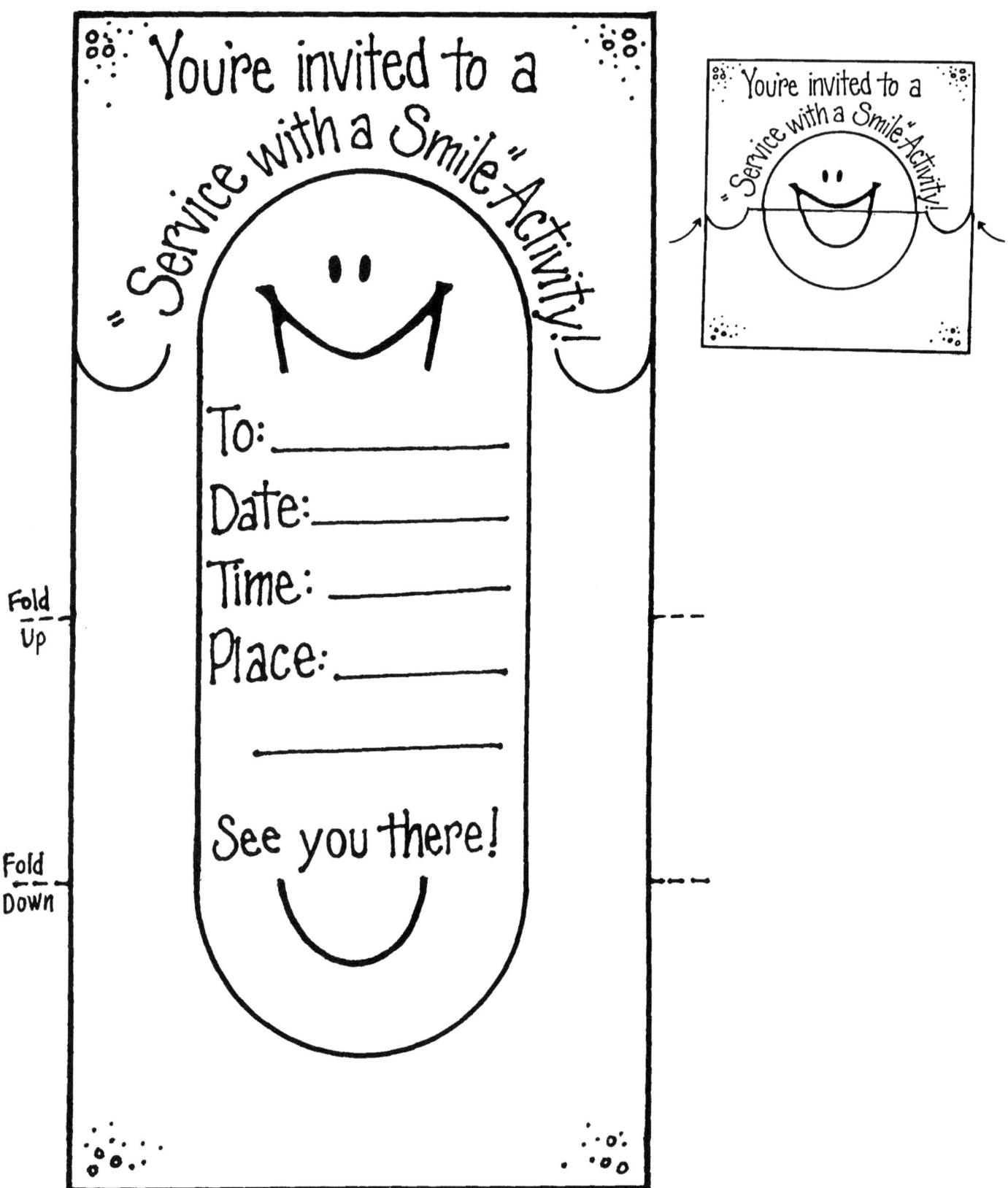

Service with a Smile: Jesus Performed Miracles

Scripture SEARCH and PONDER:

♥ Copy two sets of SEARCH and PONDER cards below on colored cardstock paper. ♥ Cut out cards.
- Use Set #1 for Daily Devotionals.
- OPTION: Make a second set of cards to play The New Testament Game--Spotlighting the Life of Jesus. (This game is found on pages 59-60 of SUPER SCRIPTURE ACTIVITIES-- NEW TESTAMENT, by Mary H. Ross and Jennette Guymon. Copy each set of cards a different color to identify quickly, i.e. copy this set tan.)

SEARCH #1
Jesus' Miracles

Jesus Healed a Man Who Could Not Walk

"On a certain day, as he was teaching ... men brought in a bed a man which was taken with a palsy ... they went up upon the housetop, and let him down through the tiling with his couch ... before Jesus. And when he saw their faith, he said unto him, Man, thy sins are

_ _ _ _ _ _ _ _ _

thee ... Arise, and take up thy couch, and go into thine house. And immediately he rose up ... and departed to his own house, glorifying God." (Luke 5:17-25)

SEARCH #2
Jesus' Miracles

Jesus Commanded the Wind and the Waves

"[Jesus] went into a ship with his disciples ... But as they sailed he fell asleep: and there came down a _ _ _ _ _ _ of wind on the lake; and they were filled with water, and were in jeopardy. ... they awoke him, saying, Master, master, we perish. Then he arose, and rebuked the wind and the raging of the water: and they ceased, and there was a calm. And he said unto them, Where is your _ _ _ _ _ ?"
(Luke 8:22-25)

SEARCH #3
Jesus' Miracles

Jesus Fed 5,000 People

"Jesus departed into a desert place ... the people ... followed him ... Jesus ... saw a great multitude, and was moved with compassion toward them and healed their sick ... and when it was evening ... Jesus said unto them, ... They need not depart, give ye them to eat ... they say ... we have ... but five loaves, and two fishes ... looking up to heaven...he _ _ _ _ _ _ ... And they did all eat, and were filled ... about five thousand men, ... women ... children." (Matthew 14:13-21)

SEARCH #4
Jesus' Miracles

Jesus Walked on Water

"Jesus ... went up into the mountains apart to _ _ _ _ ... But the ship was now in the midst of the sea, tossed with waves ... Jesus went unto them, walking on the _ _ _ _. And when the disciples saw him walking on the sea ... And Peter answered him and said, Lord, if it be thou, bid me come unto thee on the water. And he said, Come. And when Peter was come down out of the ship, he walked on the water, to go to Jesus." (Matthew 14:23-32)

SEARCH #5
Jesus' Miracles

Jesus Raised Lazarus to Life

"Now a certain man was sick, named Lazarus, of Bethany ... Jesus said unto them plainly, Lazarus is _ _ _ _. ... Then when Jesus came, he found that he had lain in the grave four days already. ... And when he thus had spoken, he cried with a loud voice, Lazarus, come forth. And he that was _ _ _ _ came forth, bound hand and foot with graveclothes and his face was bound about with a napkin. Jesus saith unto them, Loose him, and let him go."
(John 11:1, 14, 17, 43-44)

SEARCH #6
Jesus' Miracles

Jesus Healed Ten Lepers

"And ... he ... met him ten men that were lepers, which stood far off: And they lifted up their voices, and said, Jesus, Master, have _ _ _ _ _ on us. And ... he said unto them, go shew [or show] yourselves unto the priests. And it came to pass, that, as they went, they were

_ _ _ _ _ _ _ _.

And one of them, when he saw that he was healed, turned back, and with a loud voice glorified God, And fell down on his face at his feet, giving him thanks."
(Luke 17:12-18)

Service with a Smile: Jesus Performed Miracles

PATTERNS: PONDER Cards #1-6

PONDER #1
Jesus' Miracles

Jesus Healed a Man Who Could Not Walk

The men who brought the paralyzed man could not get him through the crowd of people to see Jesus.

How did they get the man to Jesus? (Luke 5:17-25)

_____ went upon the

_ _ _ _ _ _ _

and let him down through the roof.

PONDER #2
Jesus' Miracles

Jesus Commanded the Wind and the Waves

When Jesus fell asleep on the ship, what did the disciples ask him to do? (Luke 8:22-25)

CHECK ONE:

Turn the ship around ☐

Calm the seas ☐

Let down the anchor ☐

PONDER #3
Jesus' Miracles

Jesus Fed 5,000 People

Jesus used his priesthood power to change the loaves of bread and fish into baskets full, enough to feed 5,000 people.

How many loaves and fish did he have to start with?
(Matthew 14:19)

Loaves _____

Fish   _____

PONDER #4
Jesus' Miracles

Jesus Walked on Water

When Jesus walked on the Sea of Galilee toward the apostles, why were they afraid?

They thought they saw a
_ _ _ _ _ _ when they cried out in fear.
(Matthew 14:26)

PONDER #5
Jesus' Miracles

Jesus Raised Lazarus to Life

Lazarus was sick, and soon to die. Jesus was far away. By the time Jesus got there, Lazarus was dead, and in the grave four days.

What did Jesus say to Lazarus to raise him from the dead?
(John 11:43)

"Lazarus, _ _ _ _

_ _ _ _ _."

PONDER #6
Jesus' Miracles

Jesus Healed Ten Lepers

Lepers asked Jesus to heal them. What did Jesus tell them to do? "Go _ _ _ _ (show) yourself unto the

_ _ _ _ _ _ _.
(Luke 17:14)

Jesus healed _ _ _ lepers at that moment. (Luke 17:12)

How many thanked him?
_ _ _ (Luke 17:15)

Service with a Smile: Jesus Performed Miracles

Scripture Show-and-Tell

Service with a Smile: Jesus Performed Miracles poster

♥ Copy and cut out cue cards that follow.
♥ Copy, color, and cut out poster pictures #1-6 (patterns on pages 36-44).
SEE LAYOUT BELOW: All Patterns can be posted on a wall, board, or poster paper.

SEARCH, PONDER, and PLAY

**PRESENTATION PLAN:
Cards #1-6**

**Scripture
Show-and-Tell**
Jesus Performed Miracles

SHOW: Sign and Pictures #1-6   TELL: Cue Cards #1-6

Sign   Jesus Performed Miracles
Picture #1   Jesus Healed a Man Who Could Not Walk . . . . Card #1
Picture #2   Jesus Commanded the Wind and the Waves . . . . Card #2
Picture #3   Jesus Fed 5,000 People . . . . Card #3
Picture #4   Jesus Walked on Water . . . . Card #4
Picture #5   Jesus Raised Lazarus from the Dead . . . . Card #5
Picture #6   Jesus Healed Ten Lepers . . . . Card #6

♥ CUT outside line of both cards--DON'T cut center lines. ♥ Fold between center line to CREATE A FOLDER to store cards #1-6.

CUT OUT cards #1-6 to rehearse Show-and-Tell presentation.

SEARCH, PONDER, and PLAY
Jesus Performed Miracles and Healed a Man

Place Service and smile signs on board and say:

Scripture Show-and-Tell
Cue Card #1
Jesus Performed Miracles

Jesus showed us how to show service with a smile. Heavenly Father sent his son Jesus to the earth to show us the way back to heaven. He taught the people, healed the sick, and performed many other miracles.

Jesus held the priesthood, the power to act in God's name to work these miracles. Because Jesus was obedient to Heavenly Father, he was able to help and serve others.

He went the second mile to do good works. By his miracles and teachings we know that he is the Son of God.

Place Picture #1 (Jesus Healed a Man) on board and say:

There was a man who could not walk. He was carried to where Jesus was teaching and healing the people. There were so many people to see Jesus, they could not get the man who was in a bed to Jesus. So they cut a hole in the roof and lowered him down into the house with ropes. Jesus saw their faith and said unto him, "Man, thy sins are forgiven thee ... Arise, and take up thy couch, and go into thine house. And immediately he rose up ... and departed to his own house, glorifying God."   (Luke 5:17-25)

SEARCH, PONDER, and PLAY
Jesus Commanded the Wind and the Waves

Place Picture #2 (Jesus Commanded the Wind and the Waves) on board and say:

Scripture Show-and-Tell
Cue Card #2
Jesus Performed Miracles

Jesus and his disciples were on a boat in the Sea of Galilee. Jesus fell asleep and the wind began to blow hard. The waves were high and the boat filled with water. The disciples woke Jesus. They were afraid the boat would sink.

They asked Jesus to help. He stood up and commanded the wind to stop blowing and the waves to calm down. When everything was calm, Jesus asked the disciples why they were afraid. He told them they should have more faith.

They were amazed and wondered what kind of man he was that he could stop the wind and calm the waves. The wind and the waves obeyed Jesus. Why did Jesus have such a power? Because of his faith.

SEARCH, PONDER, and PLAY
Jesus Fed 5,000 People

Place Picture #3 (Jesus Fed 5,000 People) on board and say:

Scripture Show-and-Tell
Cue Card #3
Jesus Performed Miracles

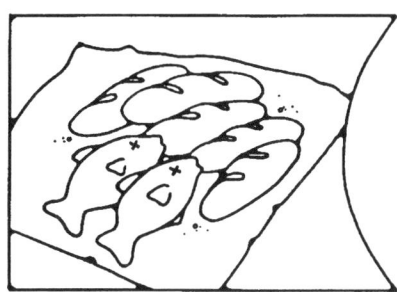

More than 5,000 people followed Jesus near the Sea of Galilee. Jesus taught the people all day, telling them of Heavenly Father's plan.

When it was night, the disciples told Jesus that the people were hungry and they should go home and eat. There was not enough food to feed 5,000 people. There were only five loaves of bread and two fish.

Then, a wonderful thing happened. Jesus told the people to sit down. He blessed the bread and fish and fed the 5,000 people. They all had enough to eat, and there were baskets of food left over. The people were amazed that Jesus had performed this miracle.

SEARCH, PONDER, and PLAY
Jesus Walked on Water

Place Picture #4 (Jesus Walked on Water) on board and say:

Scripture Show-and-Tell
Cue Card #4
Jesus Performed Miracles

When Jesus went to the mountain to pray, his disciples went out to the Sea of Galilee on a boat. A big storm came; the winds were blowing hard, and the waves were high. Jesus came down from the mountain and walked on water to get to the boat.

His disciples saw him and were afraid, thinking he was a ghost. Jesus said, "*It is I; be not afraid.*" (Matthew 14:26-27)

Peter wanted to walk on water like Jesus. Jesus told him to walk to him. Peter climbed out of the boat and began to walk on water toward Jesus. As the wind blew hard, the waves got higher. Peter became afraid and began to sink into the water. As he called to Jesus to save him, Jesus took his hand.

Jesus asked Peter why he was afraid. He asked him why he did not have more faith. Jesus and Peter then walked to the boat, and the storm stopped. His disciples honored and worshiped Jesus. They had a testimony that he was the Son of God.

SEARCH, PONDER, and PLAY
Jesus Raised Lazarus from the Dead

Place Picture #5 (Jesus Raised Lazarus) on board and say:

Scripture Show-and-Tell
Cue Card #5
Jesus Performed Miracles

Lazarus lived in Bethany. He and his sisters, Martha and Mary, loved Jesus.

Lazarus became very sick and they sent for Jesus. He told the disciples that Lazarus was dead. He told them he would bring him back to life. This way, they would know he was the true Savior.

When Jesus came, Lazarus had been dead four days. Jesus asked his sister Martha if she believed that he could make Lazarus live again. Martha said yes. They opened the grave of Lazarus, and Jesus prayed to Heavenly Father. Jesus told Lazarus to come to life again, and Lazarus came out of the grave alive.

The people knew Jesus was the Savior. They knew Heavenly Father had sent him. They had a testimony. They believed that Jesus was God's Son.

SEARCH, PONDER and PLAY
Jesus Healed Ten Lepers

Place Picture #5 (Jesus Healed Ten Lepers) on board and say:

Scripture Show-and-Tell
Cue Card #6
Jesus Performed Miracles

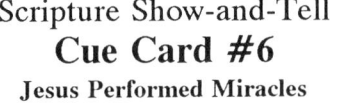

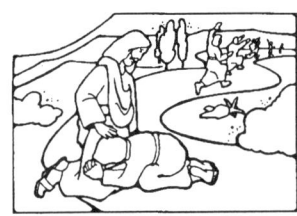

Jesus went to a small town, where he saw ten very sick men. They were lepers. They had large sores all over their bodies. Their skin was falling off. Doctors could not help them. The people stayed away from them so they would not get sick. The lepers were in great pain.

The ten lepers asked Jesus to heal them. They had faith that Jesus could make their sores go away. Jesus wanted them to be well, and told them to go the priests. The lepers obeyed Jesus and went toward the priests. On their way, the ten lepers were healed. Their sores were all gone.

<u>Only one</u> of the lepers came back to thank Jesus. He knelt down before him and thanked him for making him well. Jesus said that his faith had made him well. The other lepers did <u>not</u> come back to thank Jesus.

JESUS PERFORMED MIRACLES TO SHOW US THE POWER OF THE PRIESTHOOD, AND TO TEACH US TO HAVE MORE FAITH IN HIM AND IN HEAVENLY FATHER.

Jesus said: *"No man can do these miracles ... except God be with him."* (John 3:2)

How can we thank Jesus for all these miracles? **We can show SERVICE WITH A SMILE.**

SEARCH, PONDER, and PLAY

Go the Extra Mile:
Show Service with a Smile match game

GAME
Service with a Smile

OBJECTIVE:
Learn fun ways to serve others with a smile.

YOU'LL NEED:
Copy of match cards on pages 45-48 on colored cardstock paper for each guest, scissors, and crayons or markers

TO MAKE GAME:
Color and cut out cards.

TO PLAY:
1. Place word cards on the left and picture cards on the right face down on the floor or table.
2. Mix up cards in their separate piles.
3. Take turns picking up two cards to see if you can make a match. Watch it! These dual match cards may fool you, i.e. "I can talk to and water ..." card can match with "... Dad's shoes." Would you really want to water Dad's shoes? Or, would a better match be to water "... the plants"?

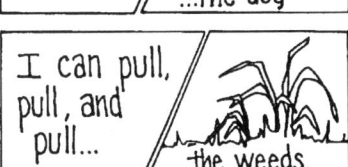

Have fun with this one. You are sure to discover
SERVICE WITH A SMILE!

SEARCH, PONDER, and PLAY

SERVICE WITH A SMILE:
Fun Choices #1-3

FAVORS or PRIZES
Service with a Smile

OBJECTIVE:
Help guests follow in the steps of Jesus by showing SERVICE WITH A SMILE.

YOU'LL NEED: Copies of Service with a Smile visor, medallion, and coupon book on pages 49-52 on colored cardstock paper, scissors, crayons or markers, glue, paper punch, metal or button brad for coupon book, and string or elastic to attach visor to head.

#1 Service with a Smile visor
1. Color and cut out visor and fold.
2. Punch a hole on each side using the paper punch.
3. Tie a string on each side of visor to tie on head. Or, use an elastic flexible string to tie on visor. Then the visor can be lifted on and off without retying string.

#2 Service with a Smile medallion
1. Color and cut out medallion.
2. Punch a hole at the top.
3. Thread yarn ribbon through hole and tie at the end.
4. Place around the neck.

#3 Service with a Smile coupon book
1. Color and cut out coupon book pages.
2. Put pages together, placing SERVICE WITH A SMILE page on top and THE END page on the bottom.
3. Punch a hole at top left and attach a wire brad or a button brad* to hold book together.

*TO MAKE BUTTON BRAD: Sew two buttons together on opposite sides of the book (threading thread through the same hole) to attach book pages.

Remember to Serve with a Smile as Jesus did.

Service with a Smile: Jesus Performed Miracles

SEARCH, PONDER, and PLAY

Service Snacks (chips and olives)

YOU'LL NEED: Copy of snack sack pattern on page 53, and snacks for each guest (potato chips, and five or ten olives each), scissors, tape, crayons, zip-close plastic sandwich bag, and Show-and-Tell cards #1-6 listed on page 29-32 for activity #2 below.

ACTIVITY #1 CHIPS: Read chips sack* and enjoy chips. Sack reads: "Chip in and help! Reach in, grab a chip, and 'chews' someone to help!" Talk about ways you might help another. Read scripture above.
*TO MAKE CHIPS SACK:
1. Color and cut out chips label, and tape label to the outside of a zip-close plastic sandwich bag (with double-stick tape).
2. Fill sack with potato chips and zip closed.

ACTIVITY #2 OLIVES: Hand each guest five or ten olives to place on their fingers. Have them name five miracles Jesus did and five things you can do to serve others.

Thought Treat
Service Snacks
John 13:34

SEARCH, PONDER, and PLAY

Super Smile Cookies (cake mix sugar cookies)

YOU'LL NEED: An 18-ounce cake mix, 3/4 cup water, 2 eggs, and frosting.
TO DECORATE SMILE USE:
1. Different colored frosting through a decorator tube, or
2. Decorator candies.

To Make Smile Cookies:
1. Preheat oven to 375° and grease a cookie sheet.
2. Beat cake mix, water, and eggs.
3. With a tablespoon, drop cookies onto cookie sheet 3 inches apart.
4. Bake 8-11 minutes or until puffed and golden brown.
5. Cool and frost.
6. Decorate a smile on top with a different colored frosting through a decorator tube, or make a smile face with decorator candies.

Thought Treat
Super Smile Cookies
Matthew 4:23-24

ACTIVITY:
As you eat, read scripture above and say, "I will serve others with a SMILE, as it's in style."

Service with a Smile: Jesus Performed Miracles

PATTERN: smile part A for Scripture Show-and-Tell ♥ Copy on colored cardstock.

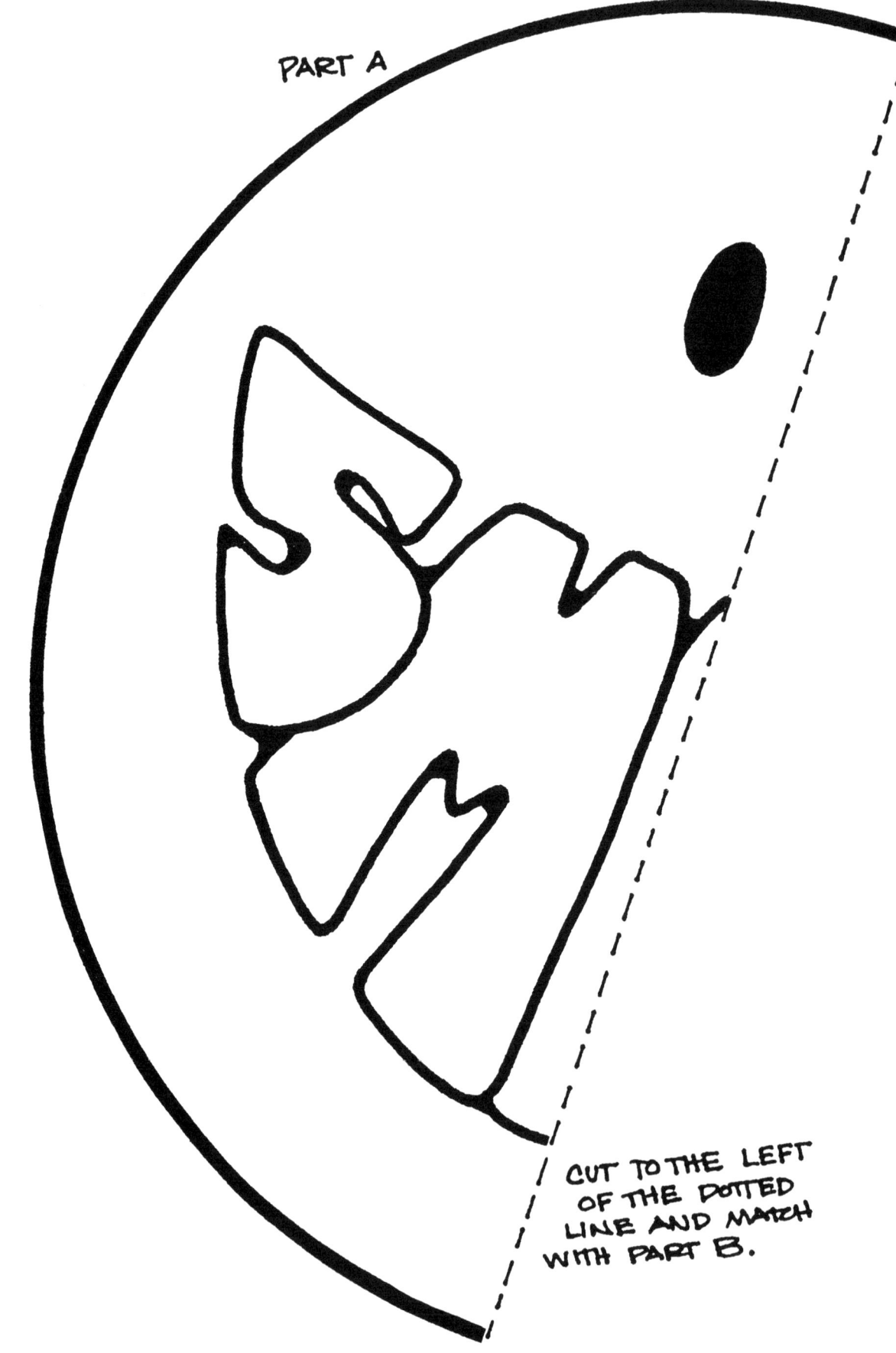

Service with a Smile: Jesus Performed Miracles

PATTERN: smile part B for Scripture Show-and-Tell ♥ Copy on colored cardstock.

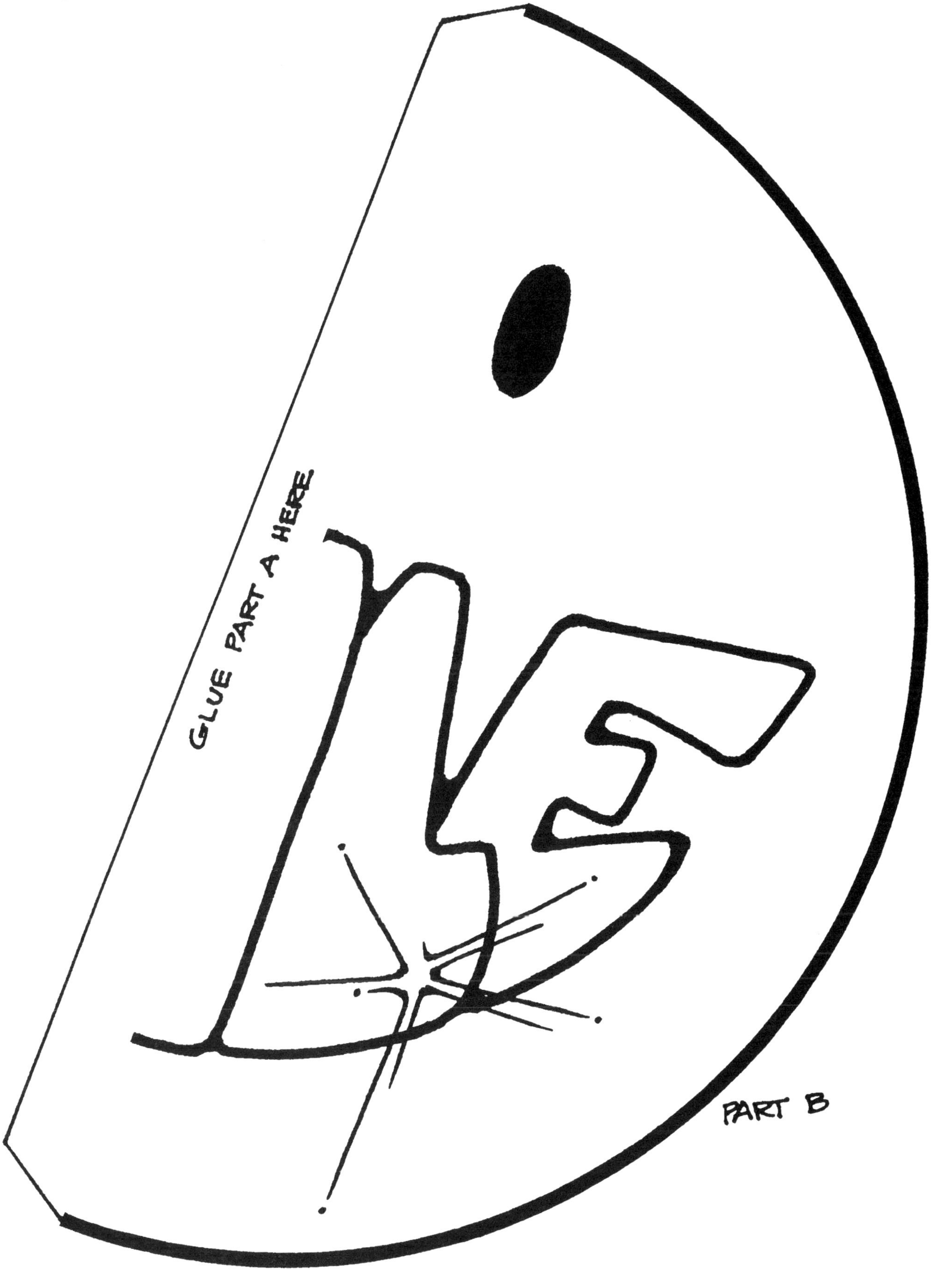

GLUE PART A HERE

PART B

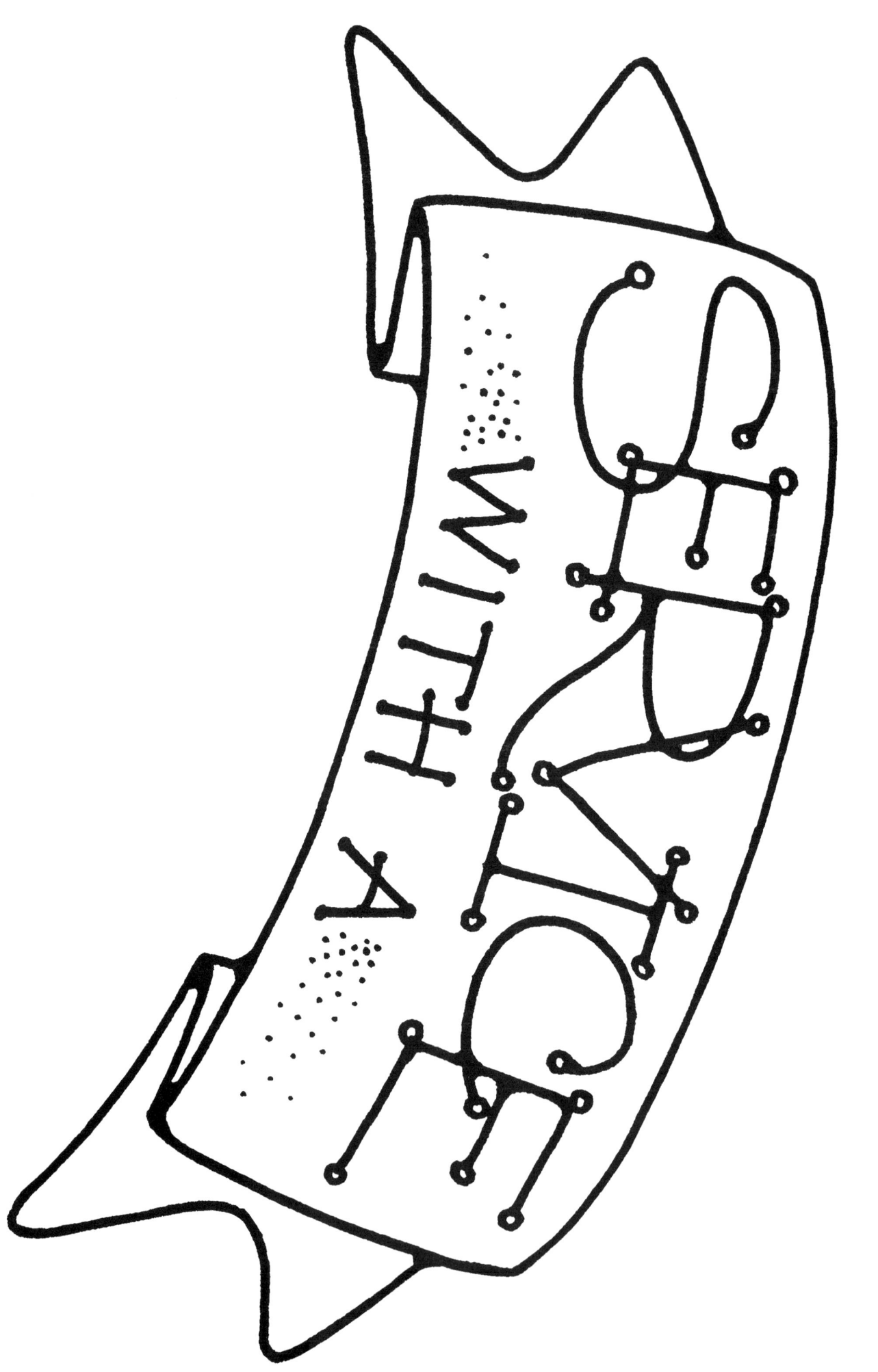

Service with a Smile: Jesus Performed Miracles

PATTERN
Picture #1
Jesus Healed a Man Who Could Not Walk --
Scripture Show-and-Tell
♥ Copy on colored cardstock.

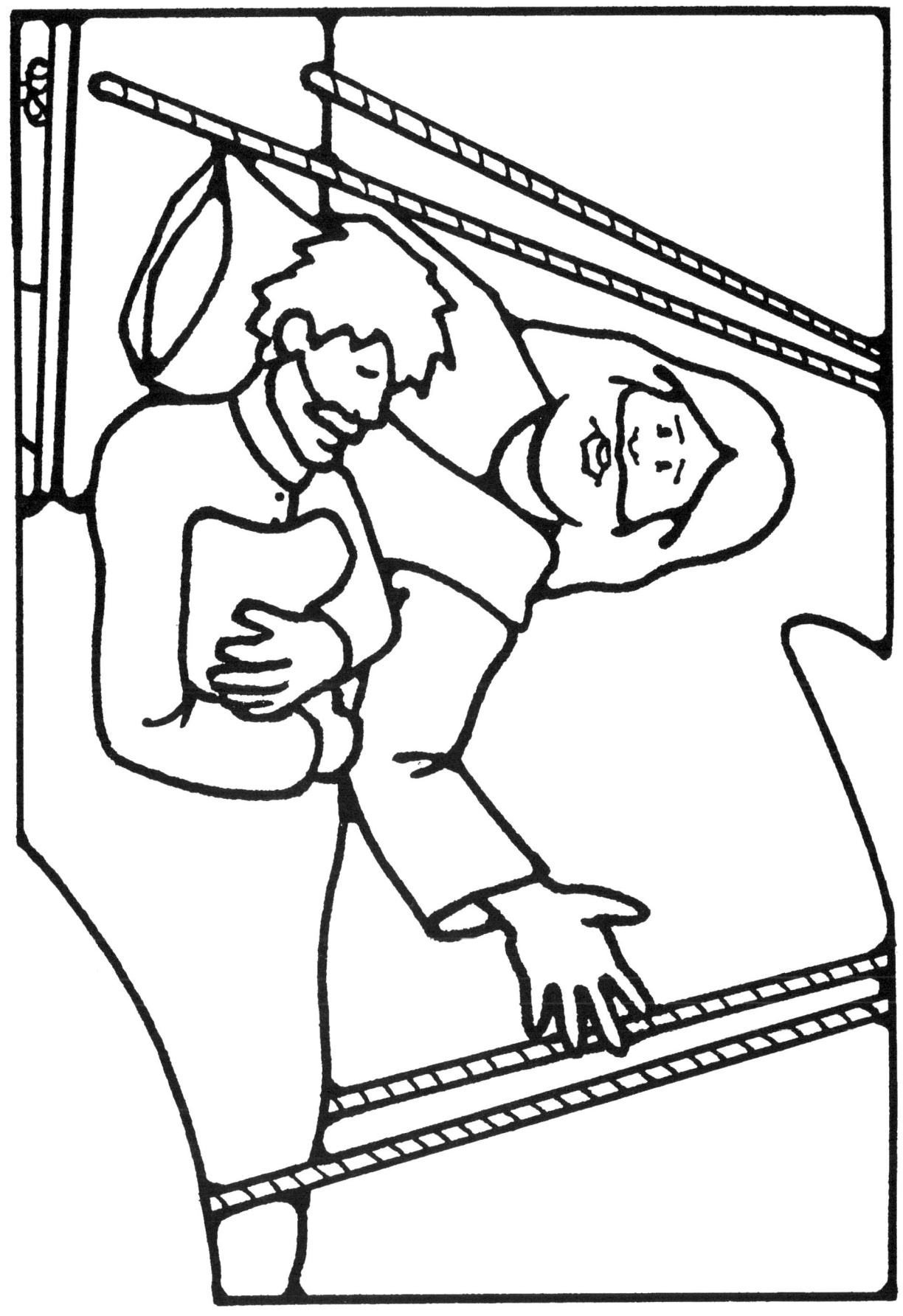

Service with a Smile: Jesus Performed Miracles

PATTERN
Picture #2 Jesus Commanded the Wind and the Waves for Scripture Show-and-Tell
♥ Copy on colored cardstock.

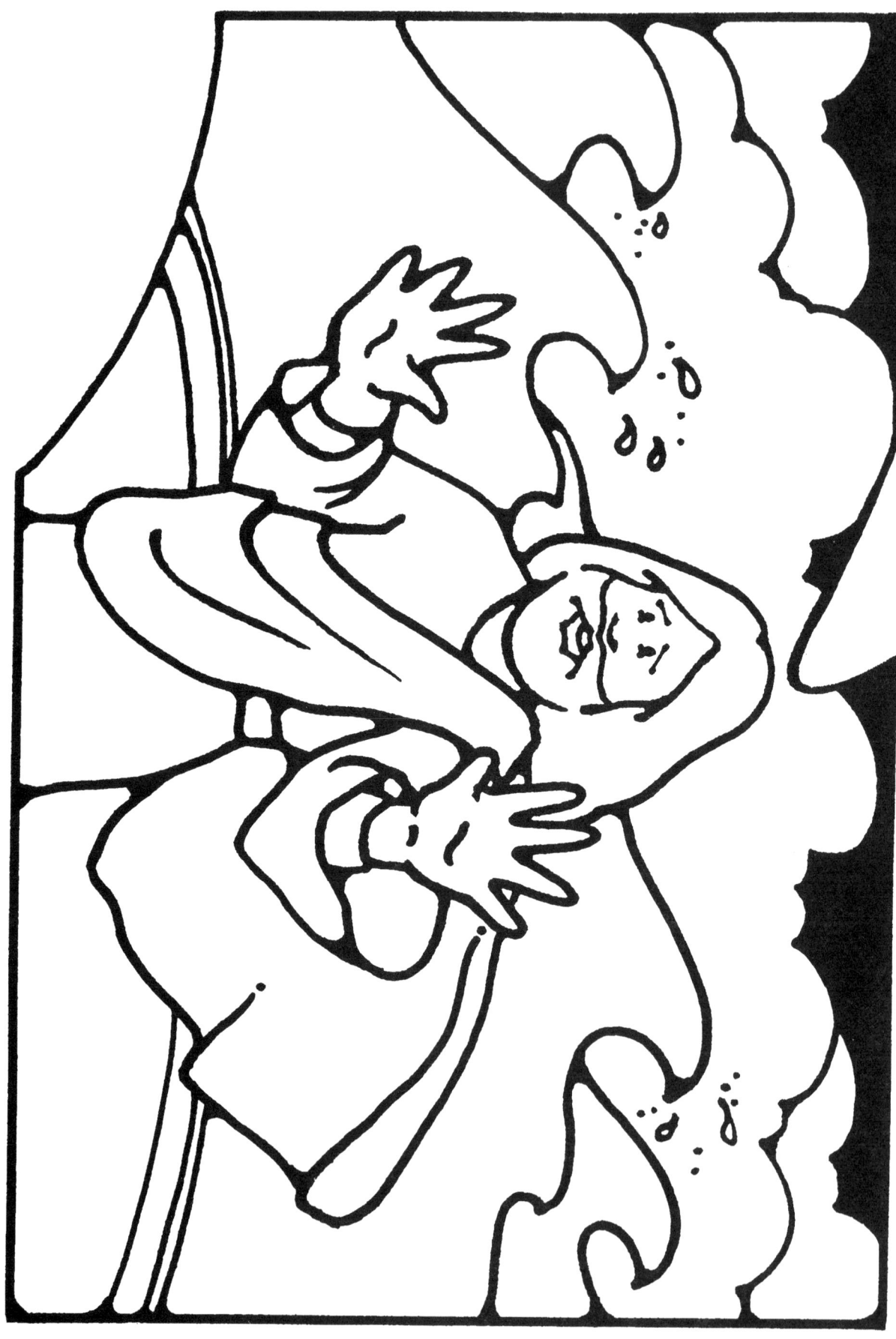

Service with a Smile: Jesus Performed Miracles

PATTERN
Picture #3
Jesus Fed
5,000 People
for Scripture
Show-and-
Tell
♥ Copy on colored cardstock.

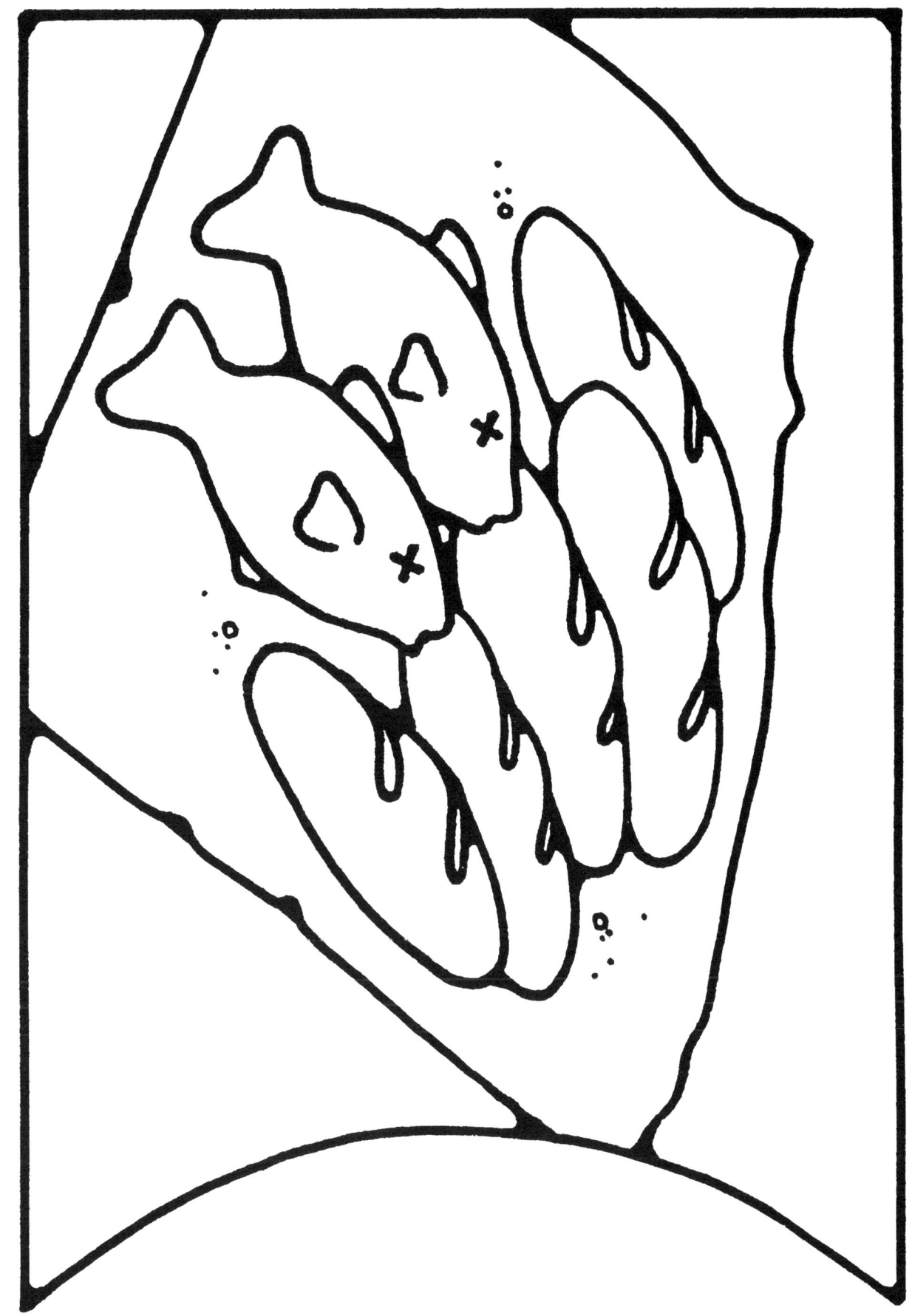

Service with a Smile: Jesus Performed Miracles

PATTERN:
Picture #4 Jesus Walked on Water for Scripture Show-and-Tell
♥ Copy on colored cardstock.

Service with a Smile: Jesus Performed Miracles

PATTERN:
Picture #5
Jesus Raised Lazarus from the Dead for Scripture Show-and-Tell
♥ Copy on colored cardstock.

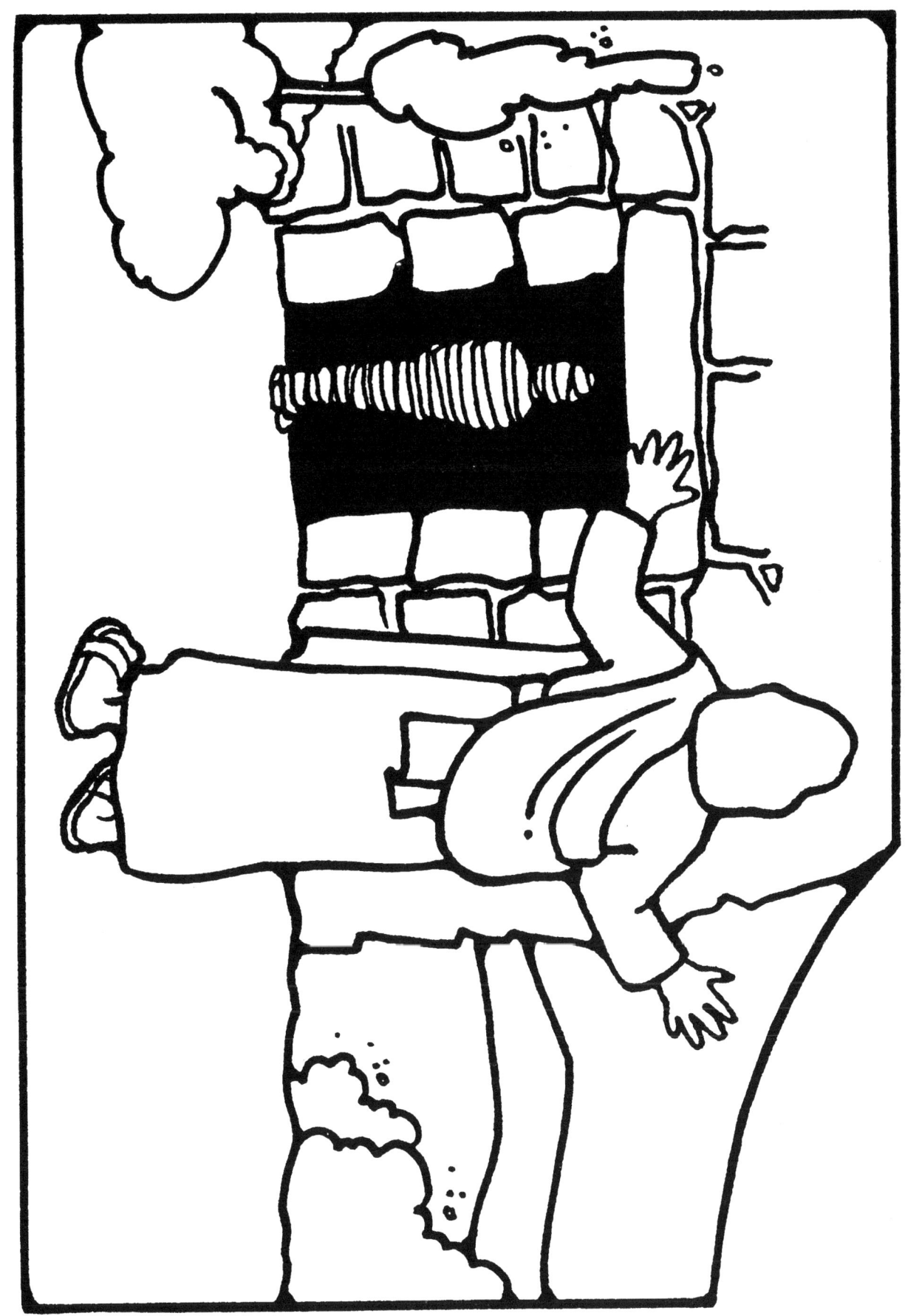

Service with a Smile: Jesus Performed Miracles

PATTERN:
Picture #6
Jesus Healed
Ten Lepers
for Scripture
Show-and-Tell
♥ Copy on colored cardstock.

I can help my brother roll... ...a snowman.

I can pull, pull, and pull... ...the weeds.

I can brush and feed... ...the dog.

I can dry and put away...  ....the dishes.

I can pick up and pack out...  ....the trash.

I can change and watch....  ....the baby.

I can make and bake for a friend... ...some cookies.

I can talk to and water... ...the plants.

I can clean and polish... ...Dad's shoes.

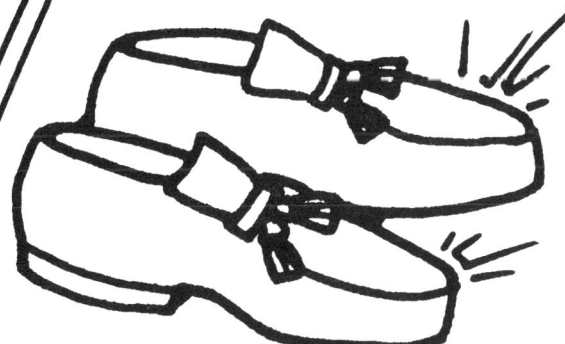

Grandma is sick so I can pick... 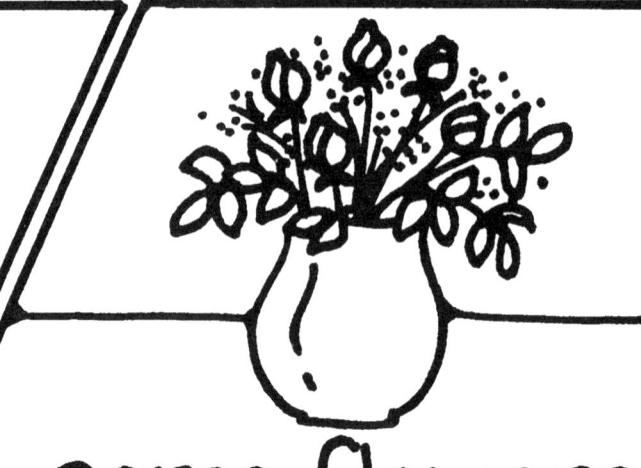 ...some flowers.

I can help Aunt Mable set...  ...the table.

I can use the broom to clean... 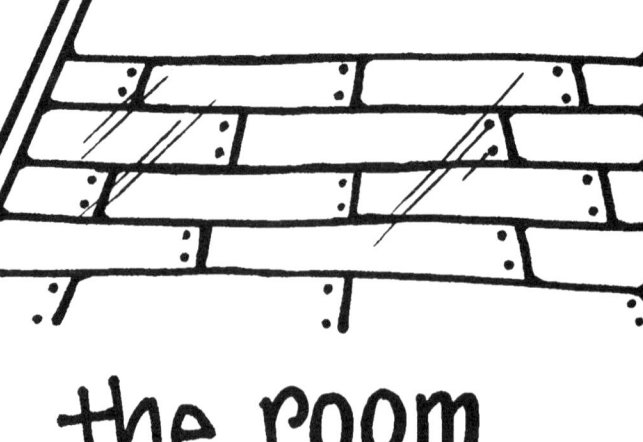 ...the room.

Service with a Smile: Jesus Performed Miracles

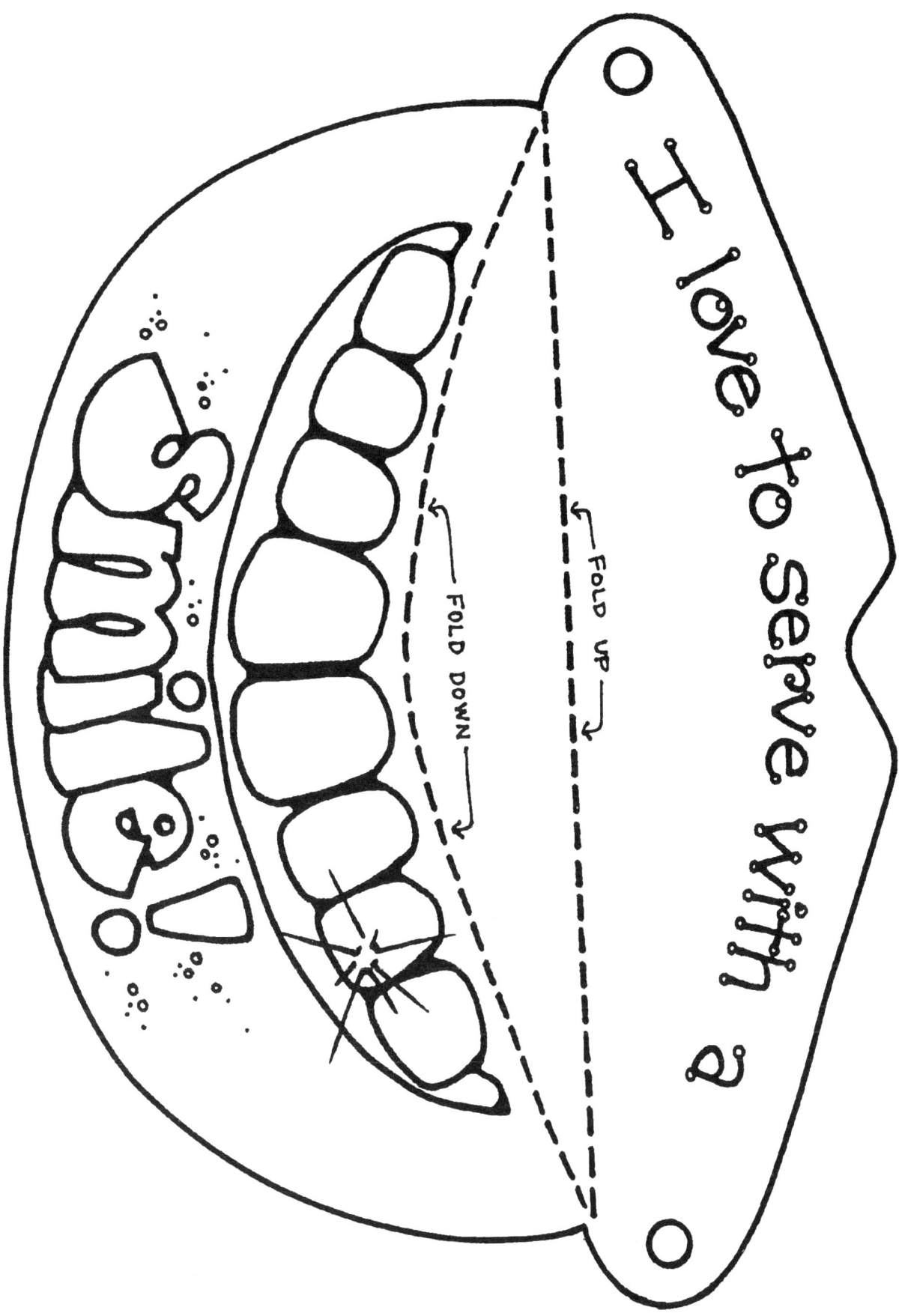

Service with a Smile: Jesus Performed Miracles

50

Service with a Smile

COUPON BOOK

Wake up you sleepy head, and I will make your bed.

COUPON: Good for the making of <u>one</u> bed.

I will take a jog with the dog.

COUPON: Good for <u>one</u> dog walk.

Here's the deal, I'll cook a meal.

COUPON: Good for <u>one</u> free meal.

☺ Mom does not adore the dirty garage floor. The cars track in dirt and leave a lot of work.

☺ COUPON: Good for <u>one</u> garage sweeping.

☺ I can help you take a look at pictures inside my book.

☺ COUPON: Good for <u>one</u> bedtime story.

☺ A kiss and a hug are on their way, when you've had a bad day.

☺ COUPON: Good for <u>one</u> free kiss and hug.

☺ I'll work all day, and slave all night. I'll show my smile. It won't be out of sight!
☺ COUPON: Good for a super smile.

Service with a Smile: Jesus Performed Miracles

PATTERN: BONUS MOTIVATORS certificate for completing the "Jesus Performed Miracles" Search and Ponder Cards and rendereing service with a smile. ☺ Copy on colored cardstock paper.

PLACE ACTIVITIES IN FILE FOLDER: Cut out and mount label and checklist on folder.

→
↓

New Testament

Captain of Our Ship:
Jesus Is Our Life Savior

SCRIPTURE ACTIVITY CHECKLIST
Captain of Our Ship: Jesus Is Our Life Savior

PAGES:

Jesus is our LIFE SAVIOR: When sailing the sea of life, we can be protected against evil. He is the captain of our ship. He knows the way back to our heavenly home. He is God's Son.

Jesus taught us how to live Heavenly Father's commandments. With his teachings we can keep our spiritual boat afloat.

DO AHEAD:
- ☐ Copy patterns 66-85
- ☐ Create Invitation 56
- ☐ Gather supplies*

Jesus asked Heavenly Father to forgive us of our sins if we repent. He died for us and was resurrected, so that we might live again. If you don't want to sink, follow the teachings of Jesus. He will bring you safely home.

We have a map for our journey through life. This map is found in the scriptures. This iron rod is the word of God that will guide us through. Read the scriptures daily to stay on the lifeboat the Lord has provided.

PAGES:

SEARCH and PONDER:

- ☐ SEARCH & PONDER cards 57-58
- ☐ SCRIPTURE SHOW-AND-TELL: Rehearse cue cards for presentation: Jesus Is Our Life Savior ship scene 59-62

PLAY: SUPER SCRIPTURE ACTIVITY Choices

- ☐ SCRIPTURE SHOW-AND-TELL presentation
- ☐ GAME: SOS Save Our Ship--Jesus Is Our Life Savior match game .. 63
- ☐ SONGS:
  - ○ "Help Us, O God, to Understand," page 73**
  - ○ "I Feel My Savior's Love," page 74**
  - ○ "To Think about Jesus," page 71**
  - ○ "When He Comes Again," page 82**

- ☐ FAVORS and PRIZES: 64
  - ○ I Can Sail Through the Storms of Life sailor hat
  - ○ My Life Can Be Ship-Shape bookmark
- ☐ THOUGHT TREATS: 65
  - ○ Submarine Sandwich with Save Our Ship flag
  - ○ Doughnut with licorice rope and Life Savior tag
- ☐ BONUS MOTIVATORS:
  - ○ Good Show Sailor! medal of honor 85

***SUPPLIES:** Pattern copies, scissors, crayons or markers, licorice rope, and Thought Treats

SUPPLEMENTAL READING--New Testament Stories**: The Savior Goes to Jerusalem, The First Sacrament, Jesus Suffers in The Garden of Gethsemane, Jesus Is Crucified, and Jesus Is Resurrected

**Children's Songbook and New Testament Stories are published by The Church of Jesus Christ of Latter-day Saints, Salt Lake City, Utah.

Captain of Our Ship: Jesus Is Our Life Savior

PATTERN: Invitation ♥ Copy on colored cardstock paper for each guest. Cut out, fill in details and deliver.

Captain of Our Ship: Jesus Is Our Life Savior

Scripture SEARCH and PONDER:

- ♥ Copy two sets of SEARCH and PONDER cards below on colored cardstock paper. ♥ Cut out cards.
  - ◘ Use Set #1 for Daily Devotionals.
  - ◘ OPTION: Make a second set of cards to play The New Testament Game--Spotlighting the Life of Jesus. (This game is found on pages 59-60 of SUPER SCRIPTURE ACTIVITIES--NEW TESTAMENT, by Mary H. Ross and Jennette Guymon. Copy each set of cards a different color to identify quickly, i.e. copy this set grey-blue.)

SEARCH #1
Our Life Savior

Jesus Enters Jerusalem: The Pharisees Plot to Kill Him

"Then gathered the chief priests and the Pharisees ... and said, What do we? for this man doeth many miracles. If we let him thus alone, all men will _ _ _ _ _ _ _ _ on him ... it is expedient for us, that one man should die."
     (John 11:47-50)
"People ... heard that Jesus was coming to Jerusalem ... went forth to meet him, and cried ... Blessed is the King of Israel that cometh in the name of the Lord." (John 12:12-13)

SEARCH #2
Our Life Savior

Jesus and the Apostles: Sacrament and the Last Supper

"And he took _ _ _ _ _, and gave thanks, and brake it, and gave unto them, saying, This is my body which is given for you: this do in remembrance of me. Likewise also the cup after supper, saying, This cup is the new testament in my _ _ _ _ _, which is _ _ _ _ _ for you."
     (Luke 22:19-20)

SEARCH #3
Our Life Savior

Jesus Suffers for Ours Sins in the Garden of Gethsemane

"Then saith he unto them, My soul is exceeding sorrowful, even unto death: tarry ye here, and watch with me. And he went a little further, and fell on this face, and _ _ _ _ _ _ saying, O my Father, if it be possible, let this cup pass from me: nevertheless not as I will, but as thou wilt. And he cometh unto the disciples, and findeth them asleep, and saith unto Peter, What, could ye not _ _ _ _ _ with me one hour?" (Matthew 26:38-41)

SEARCH #4
Our Life Savior

Jesus is Crucified and Forgives His Enemies

"And when they were come to the place, which is called Calvary, there they crucified him ... Then said Jesus, Father, forgive them; for they _ _ _ _ not what they do."
     (Luke 23:33-34)
"And about the ninth hour Jesus cried with a loud voice, saying ... My God, my God, why hast thou forsaken me? Jesus, when he had cried again ... yielded up the _ _ _ _ _ [his spirit left his body]."
     (Matthew 27:46-47, 50)

SEARCH #5
Our Life Savior

Jesus Is Resurrected: He is Our Life Savior

"The angel of the Lord descended from heaven, and rolled back the stone from the door." (Matthew 28:2)
"But Mary ... seeth two angels ... where the body of Jesus had lain. ... And she turned herself back, and saw _ _ _ _ _ standing, and knew not that it was Jesus. Jesus saith unto her, Woman why weepest thou? Jesus saith unto her, Mary. She turned herself, and saith unto him, Rabboni; which is to say, Master." (John 20:11-17)

SEARCH #6
Our Life Savior

Jesus Says Farewell, Sends Holy Ghost: He Will Return

"Being seen of them _ _ _ _ _ days, and speaking of ... kingdom of God: And, being assembled together ... said unto them [the apostles] ... But ye shall receive power, after that the Holy Ghost is come unto you ... he was taken up; and a cloud received him out of their sight. ... two men stood by in white apparel ... said, this same Jesus ... _ _ _ _ _ in like manner as ye have seen him go into heaven."
     (The Acts 1:3-4,7-11)

Captain of Our Ship: Jesus Is Our Life Savior

PATTERNS: PONDER Cards #1-6

PONDER #1
Our Life Savior

Jesus Enters Jerusalem:
The Pharisees Plot to Kill Him

The Pharisees and chief priests were jealous of Jesus, and afraid that the people would no longer listen to them. They were afraid that Jesus would be their ruler.
What did they want to do to Jesus? (John 11:47-53)

Check One:
- ☐ Throw him into prision
- ☐ Kill him
- ☐ Sell him as a slave

PONDER #2
Our Life Savior

Jesus and the Apostles:
Sacrament and the Last Supper

Jesus and his disiples met to eat the Passover dinner. Afterwards, Jesus gave them the first sacrament. CHECK Answers:

When he passed them the bread to eat, what were they to think of? (Luke 22:19)
His Body ☐   His Spirit ☐

When he gave them the drink, what were they to think of?
(Luke 22:20)
Sin Remission ☐   His Blood ☐

PONDER #3
Our Life Savior

Jesus Suffers for Ours Sins
in the Garden of Gethsemane

Jesus suffered greatly while he was praying to Heavenly Father in the garden. He prayed for all the sins of the world to be forgiven. His soul was in sorrow for all people's sins. What did Jesus ask Heavenly Father to do?
    (Matthew 26:38-41)
"Let this ___ ___ ___ pass from me [so I won't continue to suffer]; nevertheless not as I will, but as thou ___ ___ ___ ___."
[Jesus said he would keep suffering if needed.]

PONDER #4
Our Life Savior

Jesus is Crucified and
Forgives His Enemies

Did the people who crucified Jesus know what they were doing? Did they know who Jesus really was?
    (Luke 23:33-34)

Yes ☐   No ☐

How do we know that Jesus really died on the cross?
    (Matthew 27:46-47, 50)

He gave up the ___ ___ ___ ___ ___
(his spirit left his body).

PONDER #5
Our Life Savior

Jesus Is Resurrected:
He is Our Life Savior

Who came and rolled back the stone off the grave of Jesus?
    (Matthew 28:2)
- ☐ 16 people
- ☐ The soldiers
- ☐ The angel of the Lord

Who was the first person to see Jesus alive again?
    (John 20:11-17)
- ☐ John the Baptist
- ☐ Mary Magdalene
- ☐ Apostle Peter

PONDER #6
Our Life Savior

Jesus Says Farewell, Sends
Holy Ghost: He Will Return

How many days did Jesus visit with his disciples after he was resurrected? (The Acts 1:3)
15 ☐   40 ☐

Besides the power of the priesthood, what did Jesus give the disciples when he left?
    (The Acts 1:8)

___ ___ ___ ___   ___ ___ ___ ___ ___
(known as the comforter)
Jesus went up to heaven, and will return the same way when he comes again. (The Acts 1:11)

Scripture Show-and-Tell

Captain of Our Ship: Jesus Is Our Life Savior ship scene

♥ Copy and cut out cue cards that follow.
♥ Copy, color, and cut out ship and life preserver pictures on pages 66-74.

SEARCH, PONDER, and PLAY

♥ Hang ship and life preserver pictures ahead of time. Punch holes in ship and pictures #1-6 with a paper punch. Tie each picture to the matching number on the ship with a 12" or longer piece of rope string (vary lengths). Then mount ship facing forward on the board, and turn pictures facing the board. To show-and-tell about each picture, turn the picture over and tape it to the board to hold in place.

♥ When you begin, place the Jesus Is Our Life Savior picture above ship.

Scripture Show-and-Tell
Jesus Is Our Life Savior

PRESENTATION PLAN: Cards #1-6

SHOW: boat and life preserver pictures   TELL: Cue Cards #1-6

Ship	Captain of Our Ship	
Picture	Jesus Is Our Life Savior	Card #1
Picture #1	Jesus Enters Jerusalem: Pharisees Plot to Kill Him	Card #1
Picture #2	Jesus and the Apostles: Sacrament and the Last Supper	Card #2
Picture #3	Jesus Suffers for Our Sins in the Garden of Gethsemane	Card #3
Picture #4	Jesus Is Crucified and Forgives His Enemies	Card #4
Picture #5	Jesus Is Resurrected: He Is Our Life Savior	Card #5
Picture #6	Jesus Says Farewell & Sends Holy Ghost: He Will Return	Card #6

◄ CUT outside line of both cards--DON'T cut center lines. ◄ Fold between center line to CREATE A FOLDER to store cards #1-6.

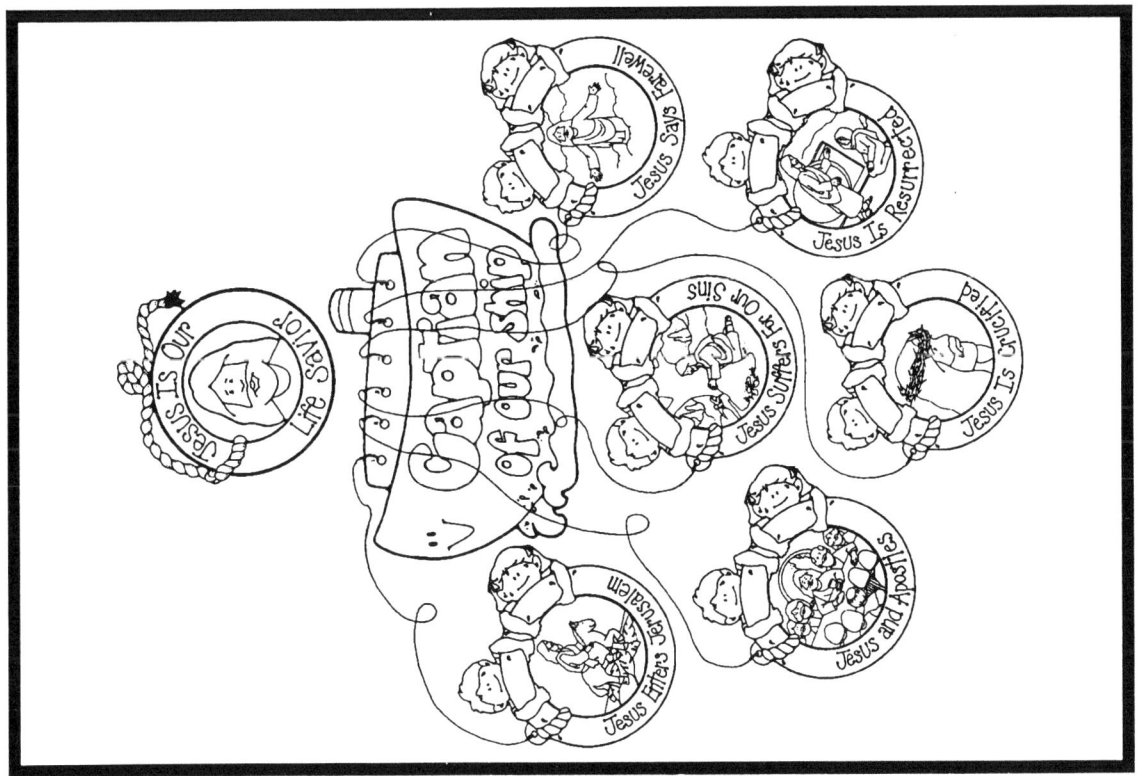

Captain of Our Ship: Jesus Is Our Life Savior

CUT OUT cards #1-6 to rehearse Show-and-Tell presentation.

SEARCH, PONDER, and PLAY
Jesus Enters Jerusalem, Pharisees Plot to Kill Him

Place ship and pictures on the board (with pictures #1-6 tied to the boat, turned face down). Tape Jesus Is Our Life Savior picture above ship and say:

Scripture Show-and-Tell
Cue Card #1
Jesus Is Our Life Savior

Jesus is our Life Savior. When sailing the sea of life, he is the captain of our ship. We can be protected against evil as we read the scriptures and learn of his teachings. We can sail safely to our heavenly home as we obey his commandments. He has shown us the way back. Let's learn how we can keep our spiritual boat afloat.

Turn picture #1 over, tape to board and say:

The disciples of Jesus did not want him to go to Jerusalem. They knew that the chief priests and Pharisees wanted to kill him. As they entered Jerusalem, the people cried out, "*Blessed is the King of Israel that cometh in the name of the Lord.*" (John 12:12-13)

Jesus wants us to have faith in him and know that his death was for a purpose. He had the power to save his own life, but he knew he had to go to Jerusalem to suffer, bleed, and die for us. **JESUS IS OUR LIFE SAVIOR.**

SEARCH, PONDER, and PLAY
Jesus and Apostles: Sacrament and Last Supper

Turn picture #2 over, tape to board and say:

Scripture Show-and-Tell
Cue Card #2
Jesus Is Our Life Savior

Jesus and his apostles needed a place to eat the Passover dinner. Jesus sent Peter and John to look for a room. The Passover feast was to remind the Israelites that God saved them from Egyptian slavery with the help of Moses.

After the Passover feast, Jesus gave his apostles the first sacrament. He broke bread and blessed it. He told his apostles to eat this bread and always remember him, that he would die for them.

Jesus poured some wine into a cup and blessed it, and told the apostles to drink it and remember him. This was to remind them of the blood he would shed. He would bleed and suffer to take away the people's sins.

Jesus told them that wicked men would kill him. This made the apostles sad, for they loved Jesus. Jesus knew that Judas would tell the wicked men where he was. Judas was one of his apostles.

Jesus wants us to remember him each week as we partake of the sacrament. As we eat the bread, we are to remember his body, and as we drink the water, we are to remember that his blood was shed. He suffered and died for our sins. The sacrament is very sacred and special.

SEARCH, PONDER, and PLAY
Jesus Suffers For Our Sins in Garden of Gethsemane

Turn picture #3 over, tape to board and say:

Scripture Show-and-Tell
Cue Card #3
Jesus Is Our Life Savior

Jesus and the apostles went to the Garden of Gethsemane to pray. He asked Peter, James, and John to wait while he prayed. He prayed for a long time, and the apostles fell asleep.

While Jesus prayed, he suffered greatly for the sins of all the people in the world. He suffered for all those who lived before him and who would live after him.

He went back to Peter, James, and John several times and found them sleeping. He went back to pray again and again. He asked them to stay awake.

He continued to pray, and suffered so much that blood came out of his skin. He shook with sorrow for the sins of the world. An angel came to help Jesus through this.

When his suffering was finally over, he came back and found Peter, James, and John sleeping. He told them that wicked men were coming to kill him.

Jesus wants us to remember that he suffered for our sins. He wants us to live a righteous life. If we do sin, he wants us to repent, pray, and ask for forgiveness. Then he wants us to choose the right.

SEARCH, PONDER, and PLAY
Jesus Is Crucified and Forgives His Enemies

Turn picture #4 over, tape to board and say:

Scripture Show-and-Tell
Cue Card #4
Jesus Is Our Life Savior

Wicked men were sent by the Pharisees to take Jesus as a prisoner. They came into the garden with sticks and swords. Judas kissed Jesus to show the wicked men who Jesus was. The Pharisees paid him for finding Jesus.

The Pharisees took him to Pilate, the Roman leader in Jerusalem. Pilate told the Pharisees Jesus had done nothing wrong. The Pharisees demanded Jesus' crucifixion. Pilate did not want trouble with the Pharisees, so he told his soldiers to crucify Jesus.

The soldiers took Jesus and beat him with whips, and made fun of him. They made a crown of thorns and pressed it down on his head, which made his head bleed. They took him to a hill near Jerusalem, laid him on a wooden cross, and nailed his hands and feet to the cross. Then they lifted up the cross, causing him great pain.

Jesus prayed that Heavenly Father would forgive the soldiers who crucified him, for they did not know he was the Savior. Jesus asked the apostle John to take care of his mother.

Jesus suffered for many hours, then he died. His spirit left his body. The sky became dark, and there was a great earthquake. The soldiers were afraid. One of the apostles took Jesus' body, wrapped it in cloth, and placed it in a tomb. A large rock was placed in front of the tomb.

SEARCH, PONDER, and PLAY
Jesus Is Resurrected: He Is Our Life Savior

Turn picture #5 over, tape to board and say:

Scripture Show-and-Tell
Cue Card #5
Jesus Is Our Life Savior

After the body of Jesus was in the tomb three days, two angels came and moved the rock away. This was on a Sunday morning.

A friend of Jesus, Mary Magdalene, came to the tomb. She saw that the body of Jesus was gone. She ran to tell the apostles Peter and John. They came and saw the cloth that he was buried in. They then rushed home.

Mary stayed at the tomb, and was crying. As she looked in the tomb, she saw two angels. The angels asked her why she was crying. She told them someone had taken away the body of Jesus.

Mary turned around and saw Jesus standing there. She thought he was the gardener. Jesus said, "*Mary.*" Then she knew he was Jesus. He asked her to go tell the apostles he was resurrected. She ran and told the apostles, but they did not believe her.

Later, Jesus came to the apostles. They were afraid, thinking Jesus was dead. Jesus asked them why they were afraid. He ask them to touch his hands and feet and feel the nail prints. They could see that Jesus was resurrected. He was alive again. His body and spirit had come together. The apostles were happy to see Jesus. They ate fish and honey with him.

As Jesus was the first person to be resurrected, many other people were resurrected too.

SEARCH, PONDER and PLAY
Jesus Says Farewell and Sends the Holy Ghost

Turn picture #6 over, tape to board and say:

Scripture Show-and-Tell
Cue Card #6
Jesus Is Our Life Savior

After Jesus was resurrected, he stayed with the apostles 40 days. He taught them about his church, and asked them to teach the gospel to all the people.

He said that he would leave soon, but he would send a comforter to guide and help them. This comforter would be the Holy Ghost.

Then Jesus went to Heavenly Father. As the apostles watched him ascend up to heaven, two men came down in white clothes. They stood by the apostles, saying that Jesus would come back someday. When he did come back, he would come out of heaven.

The apostles were the leaders of the church. Judas was dead, so there were only 11 apostles. They chose Matthias to be the 12th apostle. They held the priesthood and continued to teach the people and heal the sick. They were missionaries. People believed the teachings about Jesus, and joined his church. They were called saints.

Jesus is our LIFE SAVIOR. He is the captain of our ship. If we are to sail safely to our heavenly home, we must do as he taught. Jesus wanted us to follow in his steps--to pray often, read the scriptures, be baptized, be faithful members of his church, repent, learn of his miracles, live his parables, and teach others his gospel. This way we can live with Heavenly Father again.

SEARCH, PONDER, and PLAY

GAME: S.O.S. Save Our Ship: Jesus Is Our Life Savior match game

GAME
Captain of Our Ship

OBJECTIVE:
Ahoy Mates! S.O.S. means danger is near; have faith, do not fear. This game will help you sail the sea of life.

You can either sink or swim. Jesus is our life savior. He came to earth to save all of us from our sins.

As you read about Jesus in the scriptures, you will learn how to keep your spiritual boat afloat.

Jesus is the captain of our ship. If we listen to him, we can keep our life in ship-shape and make it through the storms of life.

YOU'LL NEED:
Two copies of each set of cards on pages 75-80.
OPTION #1 Colored Cardstock Paper: Copy each set of cards on different colored paper, i.e. copy Captain's Orders purple, and Sunken Ship cards tan.
OPTION #2 White Paper: Copy cards on white paper. These cards will be turned over in separate piles. Write the following initials on the backs of cards to identify quickly. "S.O.S." (Save Our Ship), "CO" (Captain's Orders), "SS" (Sunken Ship), "HT" (Heavenly Treasure), and "S or S" (Sink or Swim).

Captain's Orders

TO MAKE GAME: Cut out cards.
TO SET UP GAME:
1. Mix the small cards and place in a stack face down.
2. Mix large cards and give each player five. Start with less cards, i.e. two or three if more than four play.
3. Separate the remaining large cards into five different piles face down on the table. The five sets are: S.O.S., Captain's Orders, Heavenly Treasures, Sunken Ship, and Sink or Swim.

TO PLAY GAME:
1. Each player (or team) checks in his hand for matching cards. The verse must read the same.
2. Players with matched cards take turns reading their cards aloud.
3. Each player collects matched sets for points at the end of the game. Add 10 points for each card and subtract 10 points for each Sunken Ship card collected.
4. Each player lays unmatched cards in their hand face up in front of him, in categories, i.e. place all of the Captain's Orders cards together and S.O.S. cards together.
5. Players take turns drawing two small cards and placing them face up for others to see.
6. Player then draws two large cards to match the two small cards drawn. Example: If you drew a Captain's Orders and an S.O.S. small card, you draw a Captain's Orders and S.O.S. large card.
7. Player looks at his cards to make a match. If match is made, player reads matched cards aloud. If no match is made, player places the cards drawn with his other cards face up in front of him.
8. If all of large cards in one category are matched and you draw a small card with that same category, you can draw another small card.
9. When all the large cards in the center are drawn, player can ask another player for a card. It must match the small card drawn.
10. After all cards have been matched, add up points to determine the winning player or team.

CAPTAIN'S ORDERS
. . . .
CHOOSE THE RIGHT
TO KEEP HEAVEN IN SIGHT.

"If ye love me, keep my commandments. And I will pray the Father, and he shall give you another Comforter [Holy Ghost], that he may abide with you forever."

John 14:15-16

add 10 Points

SEARCH, PONDER and PLAY

I Can Sail Through the Storms of Life sailor hat

Favor or Prize
Captain of Our Ship

YOU'LL NEED: Copy of sailor hat pattern on page 81, scissors, crayons or colored markers, glue, and tape

TO MAKE SAILOR HAT:
1. Color and cut out hat and straps A and B.
2. Glue strap A to tab A on hat. Glue strap B to tab B on hat.
3. Tape or use sticky-back velcro to attach hat parts A and B around the back of the head.

ACTIVITY: Wear hats when you play the Captain of Our Ship match game on page 63 and while you enjoy Thought Treats detailed on page 65.

SEARCH, PONDER, and PLAY

My Life Can Be Ship-Shape bookmark

YOU'LL NEED: Copy of bookmark pattern on page 82, scissors, and crayons or colored markers

Favor or Prize
Captain of Our Ship

TO MAKE: Color and cut out bookmark.

ACTIVITY: Enclose bookmark in scriptures.

Captain of Our Ship: Jesus Is Our Life Savior

SEARCH, PONDER and PLAY

Save Our Ship Submarine Sandwich
(ham and cheese sandwich with S.O.S. flag)

Thought Treat
Captain of Our Ship
James 1:5-6

YOU'LL NEED: Copy of S.O.S. flag on page 83, a toothpick (to insert flag on sandwich), and a 1 3/4" piece of the submarine sandwich for each guest. Ingredients are underlined below.

TO MAKE SANDWICH:
1. Open a 16" French bread loaf and spread mayo sauce* on bottom half of bread loaf.
2. Place slices of ham and American or Swiss cheese on bottom half of bread loaf. Top with crust.
3. Cut into ten 1 3/4" slices and top each slice with a flag.

*MAYO SAUCE: 1 cup mayonnaise or salad dressing, 2 tablespoons butter, 2 teaspoons dried parsley flakes, 1/4 teaspoon dill, 1 teaspoon prepared mustard, and 1/4 teaspoon onion powder.

OPTION: Color sauce blue to look like water.

ACTIVITY: Read scripture above and talk about sailing the sea of life. Discuss how prayer can help you keep your spiritual boat afloat.

SEARCH, PONDER and PLAY

Jesus Is Our Life Savior doughnut with tag
(attach tag to doughnut with strawberry candy rope)

Thought Treat
Captain of Our Ship
John 3:16-17

YOU'LL NEED:
Copy of Jesus Is Our Life Savior tag on page 84 on colored lightweight paper, a doughnut, 12" piece of strawberry candy rope for each guest, paper punch, and crayons or markers

TO MAKE TREAT(S):
1. Color and cut out doughnut tag and punch a hole in tag.
2. Tie a 12" piece of strawberry candy rope around doughnut, and through tag to attach tag to doughnut.

ACTIVITY: Read the scripture above as you enjoy your life preserver doughnut.

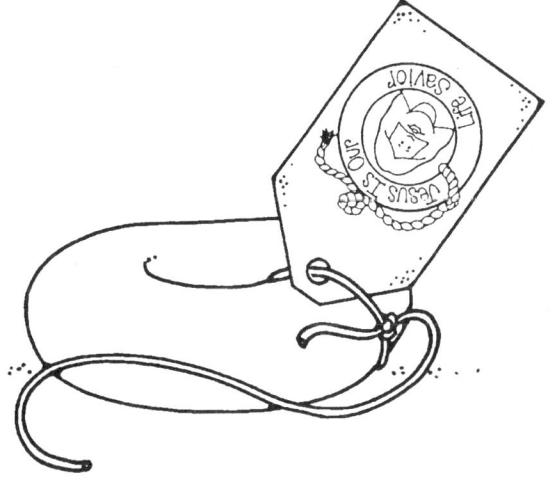

Captain of Our Ship: Jesus Is Our Life Savior

Captain of Our Ship: Jesus Is Our Life Savior

Captain of Our Ship: Jesus Is Our Life Savior

Captain of Our Ship: Jesus Is Our Life Savior

Captain of Our Ship: Jesus Is Our Life Savior

Captain of Our Ship: Jesus Is Our Life Savior

Captain of Our Ship: Jesus Is Our Life Savior

Captain of Our Ship: Jesus Is Our Life Savior

Captain of Our Ship: Jesus Is Our Life Savior

PATTERN: S.O.S. Save Our Ship: Jesus Is Our Life Savior match game ♥ Copy on cardstock paper.

NOTE: Copy this set of cards a different color from the other sets, i.e. copy this set red.

If copying cards on white paper, write the initials "SOS" on the back to identify.

Save Our Ship

S.O.S.
Save Our Ship

PRAY TO HEAVENLY FATHER.

"Whosoever shall call on the name of the Lord shall be saved."
Acts 2:21

add 10 Points

S.O.S.
Save Our Ship

KEEP GOING AND NEVER GIVE UP.

"He that endureth to the end shall be saved."
Matthew 10:22

add 10 Points

S.O.S.
Save Our Ship

FAITH WITHOUT WORKS IS DEAD.
"Ask in faith, nothing wavering. For he that wavereth is like a wave of the sea driven with the wind and tossed."
James 1:6

add 10 Points

S.O.S.
Save Our Ship

BE HAPPY THAT JESUS SAVED YOU FROM SPIRITUAL DEATH (If you Choose The Right).
"And my spirit hath rejoiced in God my Saviour." Luke 1:47

add 10 Points

S.O.S.
Save Our Ship

IF YOU REPENT AND CHOOSE THE RIGHT, YOU CAN BE SAVED.

"JESUS ... shall save his people from their sins." Matthew 1:21

add 10 Points

Captain of Our Ship: Jesus Is Our Life Savior

PATTERN: S.O.S. Save Our Ship: Jesus Is Our Life Savior match game ♥ Copy on cardstock paper.

NOTE: Copy this set of cards a different color from the other sets, i.e. copy this set purple.

If copying cards on white paper, write the initials "CO" on the back to identify.

Captain's Orders

CAPTAIN'S ORDERS

SEEK HEAVENLY THINGS FIRST, AND BLESSINGS WILL COME.

"Seek ye first the kingdom of God, and all his righteousness; and all these things shall be added unto you."
Matthew 6:33

add 10 Points

CAPTAIN'S ORDERS

CHURCH, SCRIPTURES, SING, AND PRAY--TO KEEP THE SABBATH DAY

"Remember the sabbath day, to keep it holy. Six days ... do all thy work: But the seventh day is the sabbath of the Lord thy God: in it thou shalt not do any work." Exodus 20:8-10

add 10 Points

CAPTAIN'S ORDERS

BELIEVE TO RECEIVE. PRAY TO ASK.

"Therefore I say unto you, What things soever ye desire, when ye pray, believe that ye receive them, and ye shall have them."
Mark 11:24

add 10 Points

CAPTAIN'S ORDERS

TO EVERYONE, EVEN BRANDEN, BETH, AND BAILEY, ... READ THE SCRIPTURES DAILY.

"It is written, Man shall not live by bread alone, but by every word that proceedeth out of the mouth of God."
Matthew 4:4

add 10 Points

CAPTAIN'S ORDERS

CHOOSE THE RIGHT TO KEEP HEAVEN IN SIGHT.

"If ye love me, keep my commandments. And I will pray the Father, and he shall give you another Comforter [Holy Ghost], that he may abide with you forever."

John 14:15-16

add 10 Points

Captain of Our Ship: Jesus Is Our Life Savior

PATTERN: S.O.S. Save Our Ship: Jesus Is Our Life Savior match game ♥ Copy on cardstock paper.

NOTE: Copy this set of cards a different color from the other sets, i.e. copy this set gold.

If copying cards on white paper, write the initials "HT" on the back to identify.

Heavenly Treasures

Heavenly Treasures

A DIM LIGHT IS A BURIED TREASURE; LET YOUR LIGHT SHINE.

"Ye are the light of the world. Let your light so shine before men, that they may see your good works, and glorify your Father which is in heaven."
   Matthew 5:14, 16

add 10 Points

Heavenly Treasures

SEARCH THE SCRIPTURES TO FIND TREASURES FOR HEART AND MIND.

"He shall read therein all the days of his life: that he may learn to ... keep all his words ... to do them ... that he turn not ... from the commandment."
   Deuteronomy 17:19-20

add 10 Points

Heavenly Treasures

AS YOU PRAY TO HEAVENLY FATHER, ASK FOR HEAVENLY TREASURES.

"Pray to thy Father which is in secret; and thy Father ... shall reward thee openly."
   Matthew 6:6

add 10 Points

Heavenly Treasures

A TESTIMONY STARTS IN YOUR HEART AND SPREADS TO YOUR DEEDS.

"Not every one that saith unto me, Lord, Lord, shall enter into the kingdom of heaven; but he that doeth the will of my Father which is in heaven." Matthew 7:21

add 10 Points

Heavenly Treasures

WORK FOR RIGHTEOUS RICHES.

"Wealth gotten by vanity shall be diminished: but he that gathereth by labour shall increase:"

   Proverbs 13:11

add 10 Points

Captain of Our Ship: Jesus Is Our Life Savior

PATTERN: S.O.S. Save Our Ship: Jesus Is Our Life Savior match game ♥ Copy on cardstock paper.

NOTE: Copy this set of cards a different color from the other sets, i.e. copy this set tan.

If copying cards on white paper, write the initials "SS" on the back to identify.

Sunken Ship

Sunken Ship

YOU WERE TOO SCARED TO BEAR YOUR TESTIMONY.

"For God hath not given us the spirit of fear, but of power, and of love, and of a sound mind." 2 Timothy 1:7

subtract 10 Points

Sunken Ship

YOU DIDN'T OBEY ALL OF GOD'S COMMANDMENTS.

"Put on the whole armour of God that ye may be able to stand against the wiles of the devil." Ephesians 6:11

subtract 10 Points

Sunken Ship

YOU FORGOT TO FOLLOW JESUS.

"Follow me, and I will make you fishers of men [missionaries]. And they straightway left their nets, and followed him." Matthew 4:19-20

subtract 10 Points

Sunken Ship

YOU BECAME WEAK. YOU FORGOT THAT THE SCRIPTURES GIVE YOU POWER.

"Jesus answered and said unto them, Ye do err, not knowing the scriptures, nor the power of God." Matthew 22:29

subtract 10 Points

Sunken Ship

AHOY MATES! OBEDIENCE IS THE KEY TO HEAVEN'S GATES.

"Strive to enter in at the strait gate: for many, I say ... will seek to enter in, and shall not be able." Luke 13:24

subtract 10 Points

Captain of Our Ship: Jesus Is Our Life Savior

PATTERN: S.O.S. Save Our Ship: Jesus Is Our Life Savior match game ♥ Copy on cardstock paper.

NOTE: Copy this set of cards a different color from the other sets, i.e. copy this set blue.

If copying cards on white paper, write the initials "S or S" on the back to identify.

Sink or Swim

Sink or Swim

It's the Sabbath day today, and you must decide whether to learn or play.
CHOOSE ONE:
Do you sink or swim?
☐ **SINK:** "Let's hit the pool," you say. "The sun is out and I want to stay cool."
☐ **SWIM:** You think in your mind you can swim any time, but today is the Lord's day and you will listen, learn, and obey.

add 10 Points

Sink or Swim

Your teacher asks you to stay after school. You wonder what is wrong.

CHOOSE ONE:
Do you sink or swim?

☐ **SINK:** Ditch class early, and all night worry.
☐ **SWIM:** Go see teacher.

add 10 Points

Sink or Swim

You have a problem, and the choice that is right is out of sight.

CHOOSE ONE:
Do you sink or swim?

☐ **SINK:** Ask your friends what you should do.
☐ **SWIM:** Write the problem on paper. Ask Heavenly Father to help you. Then listen to your heart for the answer.

add 10 Points

Sink or Swim

You have a math test and haven't studied. You're afraid, if you don't pass, you'll be grounded in class.
CHOOSE ONE:
Do you sink or swim?
☐ **SINK:** Coax your friend into sharing his brains. Ooops, the teacher saw you.
☐ **SWIM:** Tell your teacher that you'll have to pass, and you'll study harder in class.

add 10 Points

Sink or Swim

Your friends tell you it's the only way to go. They tempt you to smoke.

CHOOSE ONE:
Do you sink or swim?
☐ **SINK:** Try the cigarette and choke.
☐ **SWIM:** Tell your friends you'd rather go without, even if they pout.

add 10 Points

Captain of Our Ship: Jesus Is Our Life Savior

PATTERN: S.O.S. Save Our Ship: Jesus Is Our Life Savior match game ♥ Copy on cardstock paper.

NOTE: Copy this set of cards a different color from the other sets, i.e. copy this set blue.

If copying cards on white paper, write the initials "S or S" on the back to identify.

Sink or Swim

Sink or Swim

It's your father's birthday on Sunday, and you forgot to buy a gift.
CHOOSE ONE:
Do you sink or swim?
☐ **SINK:** You go to the store on Sunday and buy your dad a brand new tie.
☐ **SWIM:** You know that Sunday is not the day to shop, and you say, "Dad, I'm sorry, I forgot. If it's ok, I'll get your gift another day."

add 10 Points

Sink or Swim

Each day you say, "It's time to pray."
CHOOSE ONE:
Do you sink or swim?
☐ **SINK:** You forget to kneel and talk to Heavenly Father, who is so real.
☐ **SWIM:** You kneel each day to Heavenly Father and pray. You give your thanks and repent of pranks. You ask him to bless you and guide you to choose the right.

add 10 Points

Sink or Swim

Your parents are always on the run, and don't have time for fun.
CHOOSE ONE:
Do you sink or swim?
☐ **SINK:** Clam up when your parents are around, and forget their rules when they are out of town.
☐ **SWIM:** Make a plan and show them fun ways to be a family.

add 10 Points

Sink or Swim

Some days are crazy. There's so much work to do.

CHOOSE ONE:
Do you sink or swim?

☐ **SINK:** Say, "Work?" "I don't want to." Then join the couch potato crew.
☐ **SWIM:** Say, "I'm Johnny on the spot, afraid of work, I'm not."

add 10 Points

Sink or Swim

Money is a problem. I never have enough. Wish it grew on trees, that nice green stuff. **CHOOSE ONE:**
Do you sink or swim?
☐ **SINK:** I wait around for birthdays, Christmas and the like. I make my list and wish for things out of sight!
☐ **SWIM:** I don't depend on Mom or Dad to buy the things I wish I had. I make a list of other's needs, and plan to give, not just receive.

add 10 Points

Captain of Our Ship: Jesus Is Our Life Savior

PATTERN: sailor hat favor ♥ Copy on cardstock paper.

Captain of Our Ship: Jesus Is Our Life Savior

PATTERN: bookmark favor ♥ Copy on cardstock paper.

Captain of Our Ship: Jesus Is Our Life Savior

PATTERN: Save Our Ship Submarine Sandwich toothpick flag ♥ Copy on cardstock paper.

Captain of Our Ship: Jesus Is Our Life Savior

PATTERN: THOUGHT TREAT tags for life preserver doughnuts ♥ Copy on cardstock paper.

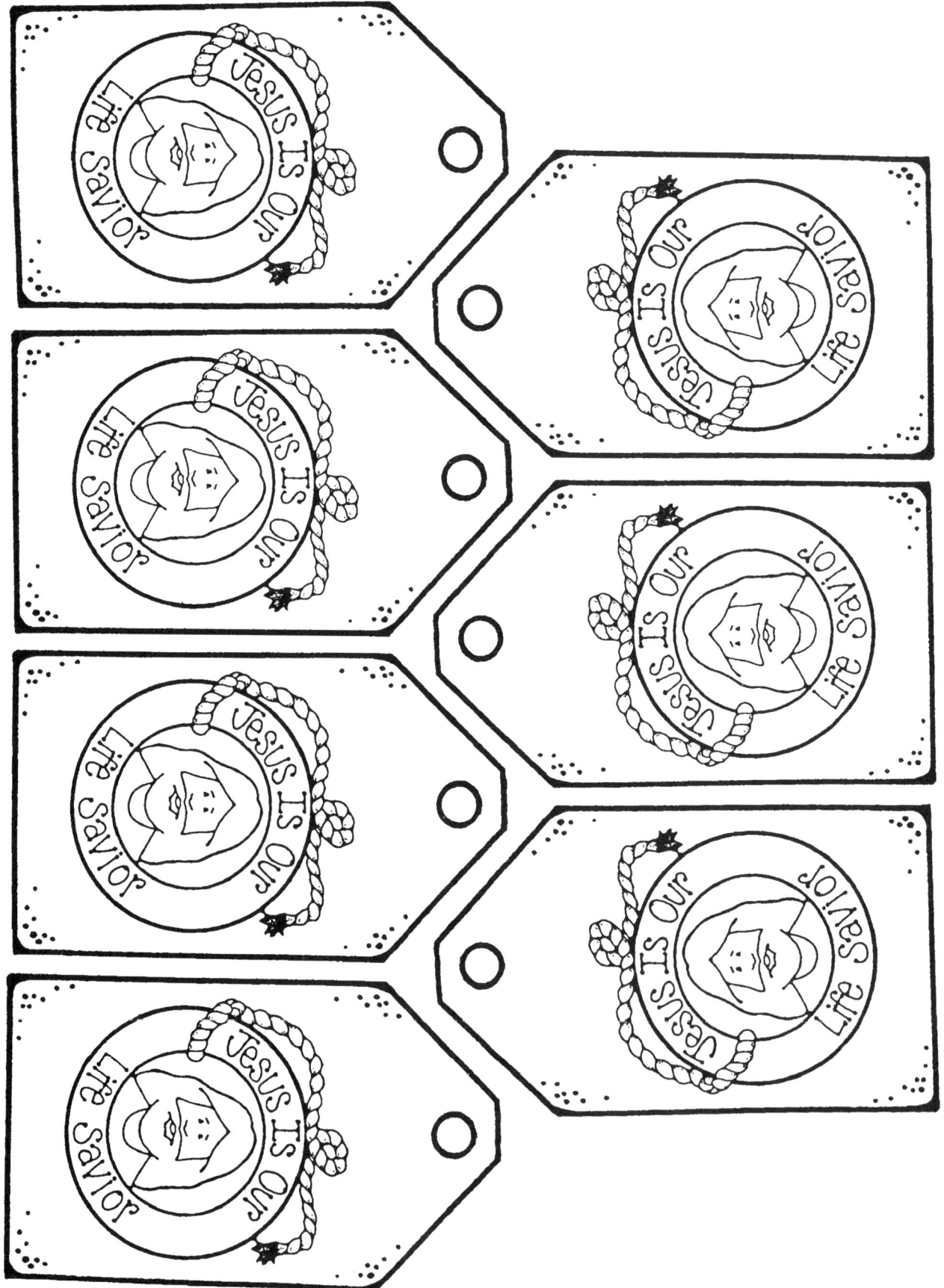

PATTERN: BONUS MOTIVATOR medal of honor (reward for completing Search and Ponder cards)
♥ Copy on cardstock paper.

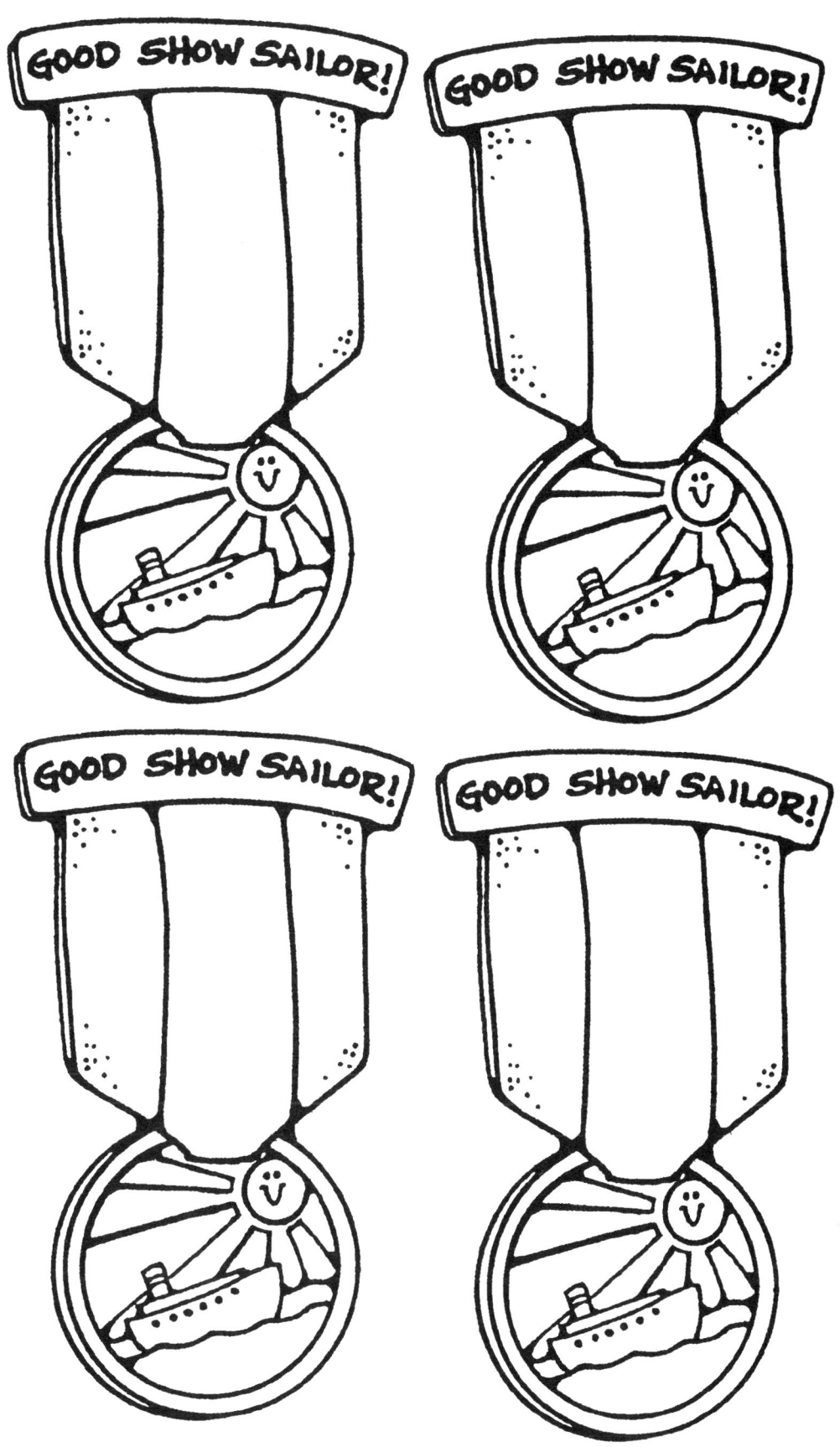

Mary H. Ross, Author and
Jennette Guymon, Illustrator
are also creators of:

SUPER SCRIPTURE ACTIVITIES:
New Testament--I'm Trying to Be Like Jesus
New Testament--Tell Me the Stories of Jesus,
(detailed below)
and
PRIMARY PARTNERS: A-Z Activities
to Make Learning Fun for Nursery and Age 3
- Nursery/Sunbeams -
(detailed on the following page)

MARY H. ROSS, Author
Mary Ross is an energetic mother and Primary teacher who loves to help children have a good time while they learn. She is a published author and columnist and has studied acting, modeling, and voice. Her varied interests include writing, creating activities, children's parties, and cooking. Mary and her husband, Paul, live with their daughter Jennifer in Sandy, Utah.
- Photos by Scott Hancock Provo, Utah

JENNETTE GUYMON, Illustrator
Jennette Guymon has studied graphic arts and illustration at Utah Valley State College and the University of Utah, and is currently employed with a commercial construction company. She served a mission to Japan and enjoys language, sports, reading, cooking, art, and freelance illustrating. Jennette lives in Salt Lake City, Utah and attends the Mount Olympus Third Ward.

Enjoy
SUPER SCRIPTURE ACTIVITIES:
New Testament--I'm Trying to Be Like Jesus

Also Enjoy
SUPER SCRIPTURE ACTIVITIES:
New Testament--Tell Me the Stories of Jesus

HEAVENLY TREASURES:
Follow the Straight and Narrow Path
SEEDS OF FAITH:
My Testimony Can Grow
IN HIS STEPS:
Spotlighting the Life of Jesus
CREATING ME:
I'm Trying to Be Like Jesus
CHOOSE THE RIGHT:
Jesus Is Our Light
LET'S CELEBRATE:
The Birth of Jesus

ANGEL TELLS OF TWO BIRTHS:
John and Jesus

FISHERS OF MEN:
Jesus Chose 12 Apostles

THE GIFTS HE GAVE:
Tell Me the Stories of Jesus

Also supplement Primary Lessons and
Family Home Evenings with

PRIMARY PARTNERS

starting with Nursery and Age 3 (Sunbeams)

How do you teach a two-year old about feelings? Can you help a toddler to appreciate the scriptures? Does a three-year-old understand what it means to be reverent? You're already well on your way to the right answers with *Primary Partners*! Children will love the dozens of fun and unique crafts and activities contained in this book. And parents, nursery leaders, and Primary teachers will love the simple, creative, memorable ways in which even the youngest children can learn important gospel principles.

Each activity is listed alphabetically and cross-referenced to a particular lesson in the Primary 1 (Nursery and Age 3) manual.

With appealing artwork and fun-to-do games and crafts, *Primary Partners* is sure to be a hit with children. Use it every week in Primary, of course . . . but don't forget family home evening, where the good times get even better.

Fun Activities to Help Your Little Ones Learn about the Gospel

- ♥ Example sandals to follow Jesus
- ♥ Moveable manger scene
- ♥ 3-D Noah's ark
- ♥ Ear-wings
- ♥ I Have "Bean" Obedient bean bag
- ♥ Tithing purse
- ♥ Bird watch
- ♥ Bug jar
- ♥ "Nature Walk" binoculars
- ♥ Giant eyes headband
- ♥ Fish bowl, fish and pole
- ♥ Smile and frown flip flag
- ♥ Hand-some bracelet
- ♥ Family face block
- ♥ Reverent church mouse maze
- ♥ Family prayer fan
- ♥ Temple tie and more . . .

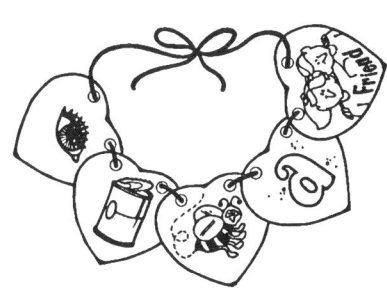